LINDA TELLINGTON-JONES

Improve Your Horse's Well-Being

A Step-by-Step Guide to TTouch and TTeam Training

KENILWORTH PRESS

Published in Great Britain by
Kenilworth Press Ltd
Addington, Buckingham, MK18 2JR

First published 1999

Published simultaneously in the USA by
Trafalgar Square Publishing
North Pomfret, Vermont 05053, USA

Originally published in the German language in two volumes:
Trainingsplan TTouch 1 and *Trainingsplan TTeam–Bodenarbeit*
by Franckh-Kosmos Verlags-GmbH & Co., Stuttgart, 1998

Disclaimer of Liability
The author and publisher shall have neither liability nor
responsibility to any person or entity with respect to any
loss or damage caused or alleged to be caused directly or
indirectly by the information contained in this book. While
the book is as accurate of the author can make it, there may
be errors, omissions, and inaccuracies.

British Library Cataloguing in Publication Data
A catalogue record for this book is available from the British Library.

ISBN 1-872119-18-2

Layout and typesetting by Kenilworth Press

Printed in Hong Kong by Midas Printing

ILLUSTRATION CREDITS

All colour photographs (including cover) are by Lothar Lenz (Cochem), except the
following:
   Ellen van Leeuwen (Klundert, NL) – page 13
   Akaka Photographic Inc. (Hawaii) – pages 40, 46, 47, 49, 52 and 53

TTouch illustrations are by Jeanne Kloepfer
TTEAM ground work illustrations are by Cornelia Koller

CONTENTS

ACKNOWLEDGMENTS 4

INTRODUCTION 5

THE TELLINGTON TTOUCHES

Using the Tellington TTouches	6
Chain, Lead Line, and Wand	8
Lowering the Head	10
Taming the Tiger	12
The Clouded Leopard TTouch	14
• *Raccoon TTouch*	14
The Lying Leopard TTouch	16
• *Abalone TTouch*	16
The Python Lift	18
• *The Combined TTouch*	18
Ear Work and TTouches	20
• *The Llama TTouch*	20
Mouth Work and TTouches	22
The Belly Lift	24
The Back Lift	26
The Lick of the Cow's Tongue	28
Tail Work and TTouches	30
Front Leg Work	32
Hind Leg Work	34

TTEAM GROUNDWORK

TTeam Ground Work	36
The Body Wrap and Rope	38
The Elegant Elephant	40
The Dingo and Cueing the Camel	42
The Grace of the Cheetah and the Half Cheetah	44
Journey of the Homing Pigeon	46
Boomer's Bound and the Peacock	48
Dolphin Flickering Through the Waves	50
• *Glide of the Eagle*	50
The Dancing Cobra	52
The Labyrinth	54
The Star, Cavaletti and Pick-up Sticks	56
The Bridge, Teeter-Totter (See-Saw), and Platform	58
Working with Plastic Sheets	60
TTEAM ADDRESSES, BOOKS AND VIDEOS	62
TTEAM INSTRUCTORS AND PRACTITIONERS	63

ACKNOWLEDGMENTS

I wish to acknowledge the following colleagues who worked with me in the creation of this book.

My deep appreciation goes to: Caroline Robbins, publisher at Trafalgar Square Publishing, whose brilliant and meticulous editing has added so much to this publication in English; Kirsten Henry for her creative input and patience while working endless hours with me on the German and English texts; Christine Schwartz for her translation from German to English; Edie Jane Eaton for her contribution and enormous attention to detail while working on the proof of the manuscript; Gudrun Braun who is responsible for the photo shoot and the German text – her perseverance made the original German edition possible; Lesley Gowers and David Blunt at Kenilworth Press, and Martha Cook at Trafalgar Square for their help with the production.

This book truly is a team effort.

INTRODUCTION

What is TTEAM training and how did the TTouches begin?

TTEAM, an acronym for Tellington Touch Equine Awareness Method, addresses the general well-being of the horse – his body, mind, and spirit. One of the basic tenets of TTEAM is to treat your horse the way you like to be treated. I have seen many rider and horse relationships transformed once this simple rule is applied in a consistent manner.

I've been developing this training system for over two decades and it continues to evolve as I learn from horses every day. My methods have their roots in classical training and I've honed these skills from the time I first began to ride. I've spent years working with many diverse breeds throughout the world and have enjoyed a wide variety of disciplines, including Western riding, show jumping, dressage, eventing, and endurance riding.

In the middle 1960s, I began experimenting with massage and physical therapy for horses and I co-authored one of the first books on the subject. We discovered we could improve the recovery of horses after competition. In the late 1970s, I had the opportunity to spend four years training in the Feldenkrais Method of bodywork for humans. It was at this time that I was struck by the idea that the Feldenkrais Method could be applied to horses. I suddenly saw horses through completely new eyes. I realized that pain, soreness, fear, and tension in a horse's body was often responsible for resistance and undesirable behavior. When I combined my experience in classical training and the Feldenkrais Method the result was the foundation of TTEAM work. I found it possible to change behavior and influence personality without force or constant repetition by using non-habitual, non-threatening movements of the horse's body and special ground exercises.

Several years later, my interest in cellular intelligence and equine massage led me to advance my training method by adding the Tellington TTouch. The TTouch influences the nervous system, instigates learning by activating the body's cells, integrates body and mind, and, as a result, encourages a state of health. I feel the TTouch has a magical dynamic – as though it's a secret, wordless language between you and your horse.

The TTouch is a series of circular touches made with the hands and fingers intended to activate cellular function and to further deepen understanding and communication between horse and human. For each TTouch, hands and fingers are held in different positions and applied with varying pressures, depending upon the response of the horse and the desired effect.

TTEAM ground exercises influence behavioral and physical problems by dramatically expanding a horse's awareness and improving his balance, coordination, willingness, and ability to learn. This book will lead you through the basic TTouches and TTEAM ground work. It will give you new tools for training and healing horses for optimum performance and health, and best of all, it will help you develop a very special bond between you and your horse.

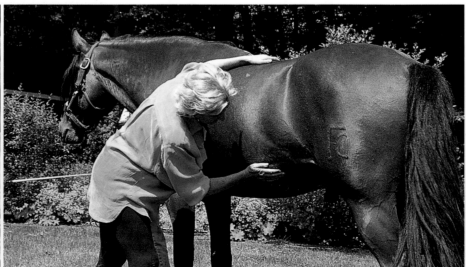

USING THE TELLINGTON TTOUCHES

The TTouches encourage and increase relaxation, improve athletic ability, and accelerate a horse's ability to learn.

GETTING STARTED WITH BODY EXPLORATION

Before you learn the individual TTouches, you need to explore your horse's body to find the areas of sensitivity, tension, or soreness. You do this by running your hands over the body and observing any physical symptoms of discomfort or distress – such as throwing the head, or swishing the tail – from the pressure of your hand or fingers. These reactions will indicate to you the areas that need addressing with TTouches. Do not tie your horse, but have someone hold him for you in case he throws up his head, or moves abruptly.

Begin with a "soft", flat hand and use long, slow strokes to explore his entire body. Be sensitive for heat, cold, swelling, lumps, changes in muscle tone, differences in hair quality, and indications from him that he may be concerned about what you are doing.

Next, do a deep fingertip exploration on the spots marked in the drawing to search for sore, tender, or "fearful" areas. Hold your fingers together, with the fingertips "hooked". To explore the body, start at the neck in the middle of the large muscles just behind the ears. Stroke him with the flat of your hand first so you don't surprise him, then press straight into the muscle with your fingertips and release instantly. To explore most horses, begin with a number four pressure (except on a horse who is nervous or spooky, when you should begin carefully with a number three pressure), then you can increase or decrease the pressure to discover which gives you the most information about the degree of his sensitivity or stability. Some sensitive horses will react to a number two pressure, and some very relaxed ones may react only to a higher pressure. You may get a strong response at first because the horse is not expecting the sensation, so always repeat the pressure to be sure the resulting reaction is not from surprise.

Move down the neck, and to the shoulders, then to the sides. Be careful to watch for your horse's response, which if your horse is very sensitive, or sore, could be throwing his head up and stepping back, moving away, holding his breath, or threatening with a kick or a bite. This is his way of "talking" to you, so listen and always be alert. As a generality, expect a healthy horse with no soreness or tension in any given area, to show a slight response to a number five pressure, but no spasm or fear. If your horse shows very little, or no response, he may be a quiet, steady type, or you may be pressing and releasing with the pads rather than the tips of your fingers. Of course, the best way to learn how to evaluate the degrees of muscle tension and sensitivity is to explore many horses and gauge their response to your pressure.

THE TTOUCH PRESSURE SCALE

• The TTouch pressure ranges on a scale from one to nine. To understand what a *number one pressure* is, place your thumb against your cheek. With the tip of your middle finger, push the skin on your eyelid in a one and a quarter circle with the lightest contact possible. Make sure you move the skin, and are not just sliding over it. Repeat this movement on your forearm, observing how small an indentation you make in the skin. This is a number one pressure. (With these eyelid tests, use caution if you wear contact lenses).
• To discover a *number three pressure*, make several slightly firmer circles on your eyelid that still allow you to feel safe and comfortable. Repeat this circular pressure on your forearm, noting the depth and pressure of the indentation. This number three pressure should still be very light.
• A *number six pressure* on your forearm should be twice as deep as the number three pressure. Tip the first joint of the fingers so that your fingernails are pointing directly into the muscle of your arm.
• For a *number nine pressure*, which is used only occasionally, apply three times as deeply as the number three pressure.

THE CIRCLES FOR THE BASIC TTOUCH

The foundation for the TTouch is a circular movement called the Clouded Leopard TTouch (page 14). It is the first TTouch we teach because the techniques and principles used are basic to all the circular TTouches. (You may be wondering why the TTouches and many of the ground work exercises have been named after various animals rather than just given numbers. Well, all animals inspire me, so we have named each TTouch or leading position after a specific animal – some of them give us a quick visual image of what that exercise represents. I know it is an unusual and unique connection to the animal kingdom, but I hope it adds some smiles and laughter to TTEAM work, and some much needed fun and humor into the overly serious horse world!)

Begin by orienting yourself: imagine the face of a coin roughly the size of a quarter (10p) anywhere on your horse's body. With your left hand placed lightly on your horse, take your right hand and place your fingers at six o'clock on the bottom of the circle of your imaginary dial. With your fingers held in a lightly curved position like a paw, push the skin around the face of our imaginary clock in a circle and a quarter, then release. If your horse seems relaxed, bring your fingers away softly and begin again at another spot chosen at random.

We often place the circles at random for the first few minutes as a way of keeping the horse focused. He will remain in a state of attention because he is wondering where the next move will come from. Because each circle is a complete movement within itself, you can work the body in any order you wish without losing effectiveness.

Once your horse accepts the TTouch, follow a line running parallel to your horse's topline and connect each circle with a light slide about two inches between circles (see drawing).

It's important to make only one circle and a quarter on any one spot at a time. Many people learning the TTouch for the first time, keep

circling in the same place, and this usually has the effect of irritating the horse. Keep the circles really round and make them in one smooth, flowing movement. Breathe rhythmically and slowly, and stand in a safe position, with your feet hip-width apart, making sure your knees are not locked.

If, when you make your initial circles, your horse moves around, make the circles fairly fast, taking about one second to make each circular motion. As your horse begins to trust and enjoy what's happening, slow each circle down to approximately two or three seconds. To complete this slower circle, instead of simply lifting off when you reach eight o'clock, pause, and allow your fingers to come up in a gradual release, as though a sponge were slowly pushing them up and away from the body. Then slide to the next circle.

WHY USE THE TTOUCH ON HORSES WITH NO PROBLEMS?

The TTouches are not just for horses with physical or behavioral problems, but provide horse people of all levels with a humane, logical, and effective way of supporting most training methods. They can be used to encourage and increase relaxation, improve athletic ability, introduce a new sense of awareness, reduce stress in performance horses, accelerate a horse's ability to learn, facilitate the work of farriers and vets, and in general make horses more willing to give us their attention.

CHAIN, LEAD LINE, AND WAND

The combination of the two main tools used in TTEAM work, the chain lead line (a lead line with a portion of chain with a clip at one end), and the wand, gives you maximum control over your horse, at the same time keeping him light, soft, and well-balanced.

What do you need?

- A well-fitting leather or nylon halter with rings.

- A six-foot nylon lead line with a thirty-inch chain attached.

- A four-foot long, stiff, preferably white, dressage whip – called the wand.

Remember...

Although use of a chain is sometime controversial because people have seen it used abusively, the chain lead line is a wonderful tool when used properly, and will teach your horse to respond to clear, light signals on his halter (in preparation for rein aids), but only use it in combination with the wand and your voice. Never tie your horse with it.

The Zephyr Lead

If you feel unsure about using a chain, or have a young or very sensitive horse, try using a lead line fitted with a soft rope in place of the chain.

HOW TO PUT THE LEAD LINE ON

1 First, adjust the halter so the noseband is sitting about three fingers width below the protruding cheekbones.(British readers please note that in America we call a headcollar a halter, so don't be confused.) These instructions assume that the handler is on the left since most horses are led from that side, however remember that if you lead your horse from both sides he will learn to be more flexible under saddle.

2 Run the chain from the outside left downward through the lower ring on the halter..

3 Lift the chain up so it crosses over the noseband of the halter – not directly on the horse's nose. Take it out through the lower right halter ring.

4-5 Attach the snap at the end of the chain on the upper right ring of the halter. If the chain is too long, pull the snap through this ring and fix it back on itself on the chain. You need to have about four to six inches of chain left over on the side you are leading from.

If your horse is naturally high-headed, or throws his head up and is resistant to lowering it, just fasten the chain up the side of the halter as shown in the head-lowering pictures on the next page. This method of fastening the chain encourages horses to lower their head much more willingly. When the head is lower you can shorten the chain with this figure-eight system as shown in the drawing.

The Wand

- Some people take exception to a whip being called a wand, but it is done so in TTEAM for a couple of reasons. First, instead of thinking of the whip as something with which to punish, we use it as an extension of our arm and as another way to clearly signal our wishes. Second, it is magical in the way it focuses an animal almost immediately. You can calm a nervous horse, or teach a slow or lazy horse to go forward.

- To move your horse forward in the walk: use the wand to stroke his back and croup firmly two or three times, then tap him on the croup at the same time as you give a slow voice command to walk, and a forward signal and release on the chain.

- To stop your horse, tap his chest lightly three times, at the same time as you give a slow "whoaaa" and a signal and release on the chain.

LOWERING THE HEAD

High-headed means high strung! Encouraging your horse to lower and maintain an effective head position without force, pain, or anxiety overrides his instinct to flee. Feeling more secure, his physical, emotional and mental balance will improve.

Why do it?

In addition to making the horse feel more secure by overriding his flight, fight, or freeze reflex, it relieves muscle tension in the neck and back, encourages rhythmical breathing, and makes the horse much easier to handle for the vet and farrier, clipping, acupuncture and chiropractic treatments.

Remember…

The ideal position for the horse's head is when his poll is approximately four inches lower than his withers. If the head gets too low, he might just relax a bit too much – "go to sleep" – and not pay attention to you at all.

LOWERING THE HEAD

1 Place one hand on the noseband and the other on the horse's crest quite close to his poll. With a light pressure on the noseband and using the Clouded Leopard TTouch (page 14) on his crest ask him to lower his head. It helps with some horses if you gently rock their head and neck from side to side a little as you ask for the lowering. If these methods don't work, try the next steps.

2-3 Thread the chain part of the lead line up the side of the halter instead of over the nose. Stroke the horse's neck, chest, and legs down to the ground while asking him to lower his head with a light "ask and release" signal on the chain.

4 If he still will not cooperate, squat down and bend your upper body forward. (Make sure you squat slightly off to the side – not right in front – for safety). Your body language should encourage the horse to lower his head. When he does so, stand up slowly, keeping his head down. It is common for some horses who are tense, or particularly high-headed, to take a few steps forward when you first ask them to lower their head. Prevent them from doing this by stroking their chest with the wand to discourage them from wanting to move forward.

Lowering the head from the front

Stand in front and lightly place both hands on his noseband. Hold it with slightly curved, open fingers. Do not hold it tightly in case he throws his head up, in which case your fingers may get caught. Press lightly downward on the noseband, and then release. If he doesn't lower his head, use one hand to hold the lead line down, while the other presses downward on the noseband.

Linda's tip

When you are riding and you want your horse to lower his head you can use the Clouded Leopard TTouch (page 14). Reach out and do the TTouch on the crest of his neck close to his poll.

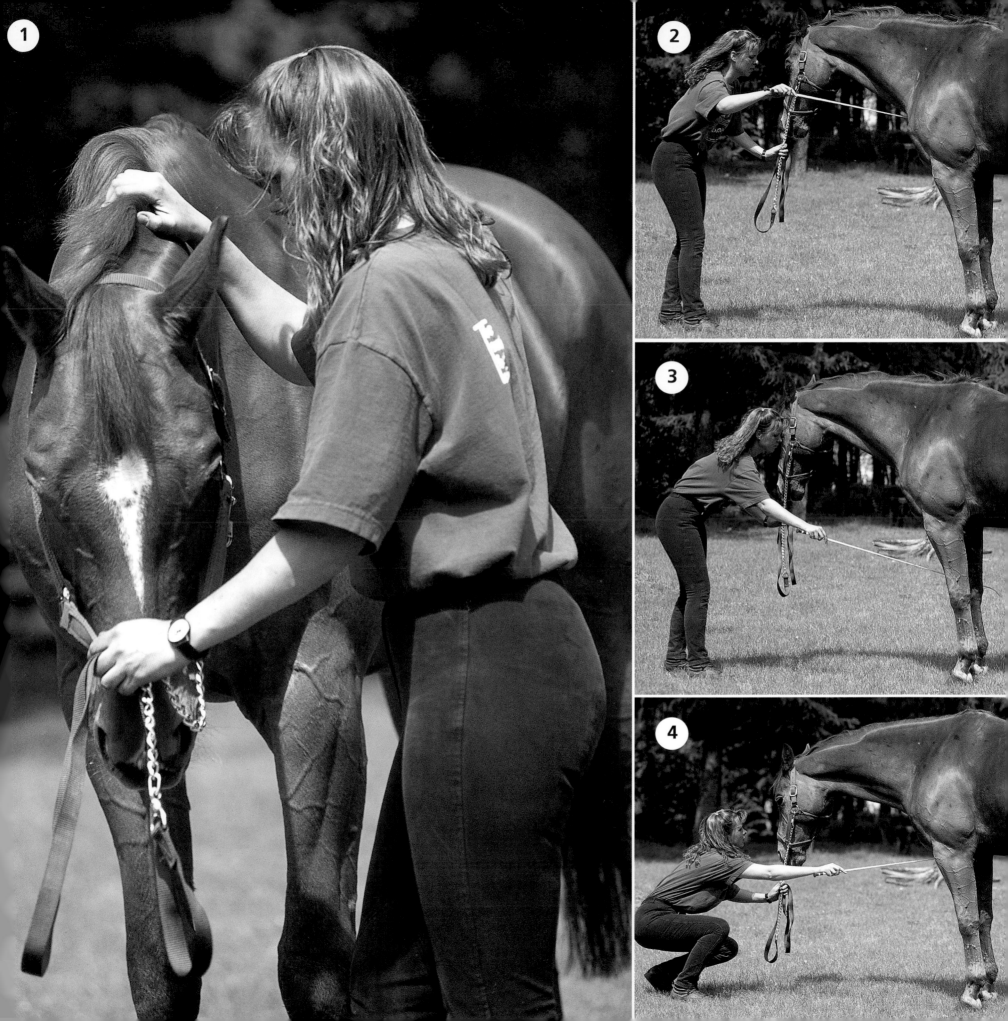

TAMING THE TIGER

Taming the Tiger is a "half" cross-tie position. It is extremely effective for teaching patience and self-control, and prepares a horse to stand alone in a regular cross-tie.

Why use it?

It is an essential tool to use with a horse who cannot stand still for the vet or the farrier, or who paws the ground, kicks, or bites when you are trying to work on him, and you don't have an extra handler around. It is also very useful for teaching a horse to be tied.

Linda's tip

If your horse will not stand still for bodywork, keep a steady contact on both lines, so he cannot move around too much. Do not get annoyed with him, just stay calm. When he responds, and stands quietly, loosen the contact slowly so his head is free again.

Remember...

If your horse can turn to watch you TTouching, or grooming him, he can be a participant in the process rather than being required to submit to whatever you do. Having his head free makes it easier for him to give, and for you to perceive the small indicators which should let you know the concerns he may have about what you are doing. If you are unable to hear his "whispers", he may have to "scream" at you with teeth and heels.

TAMING THE TIGER

1 Place your horse parallel to a wall or fence where you can run the line through a ring, or around a post or bar at the height you would like your horse to hold his head.

2 If you think your horse might pull back, attach the chain on the side of the halter in one of the two configurations described below.

3 Thread the rope away from you through the halter ring behind the horse's chin. Run it through the ring on the wall, or behind the post or bar, and tie it back to the lower side ring of the halter with a quick-release knot.

4 Hold the rope and lead line in one hand – separated by your index finger (see photo below). In this way you will have the other hand free to stroke with the wand, or do TTouches. The wand is also very important to help reposition the horse if he moves. To adjust the position of the horse's head sideways in either direction you need to lengthen one line as you shorten the other. For this, the rope must be able to slide around the post, or through the ring in the wall.

What do you need?

- A safe place to tie your horse in a corner.

- A lead line with a chain.

- A fifteen-to-twenty-foot long rope.

- A four-foot long, stiff whip (the wand).

What you should do if ...

• Your horse pulls back

Find a place to tie him where he has a solid barrier a few steps behind him. When he pulls back, release the rope and then stroke and tap his hindquarters with the wand to encourage him to come quietly forward. With nothing to pull against he will probably stop pulling back immediately. When he comes forward, take a clearer hold on the rope again. (It is apparent that pressure on the poll triggers many horses to pull back and it is an instinctive response they need to learn to override. Anyone who has tried to help a foal to suckle by pushing its head under the mare will know the frustration of having them push up against the hand rather than go down for the food!).

• You do not have a smooth fence to put the rope around

The rope must be able to move and slide, so tie it to a metal ring attached to the fence, post, or wall.

• Your horse goes backward when tied

Find a place to tie him where he physically cannot back up more than two steps. Use the Dingo leading position (p.42) to ask him to come forward.

THE CLOUDED LEOPARD TTOUCH

The Clouded Leopard is the basic TTouch position. It increases a horse's self-confidence, and can help back pain, tension, muscle pain, over-sensitivity, as well as reducing stress.

Remember…

If you need to put some energy into your horse, do this TTouch fast. This means doing the one and a quarter times around the circle in approximately one second. If you want to achieve the opposite effect and relax him, do the circles slowly – taking about three seconds to complete each circle.

Linda's tip

You can build trust by applying the Clouded Leopard TTouch (and the Raccoon TTouch described below) on your horse's forehead. Try this on the horse who is hard to catch, or the one who won't stand still for mounting. Or, just do it on horses who are frightened, tense, or generally over-sensitive.

Which parts of the body?

CLOUDED LEOPARD TTOUCH

1 Hold your hand gently curved and use the pads of your fingers close together. In the drawing the shaded areas indicate the parts of the fingers which should be in contact with the horse. Place your other hand a comfortable distance away somewhere else on the horse's body to keep the connection between your hands, and help you with your balance. Be sure that the resting hand is on an area where the horse feels safe about being touched. Breathe calmly and rhythmically. The horse will mirror your relaxation, and your even breathing will help you keep your hands, fingers, arms, and shoulders, soft and moveable.

2 Push the skin one and a quarter times clockwise around a half-inch diameter circle, and slowly release. Imagine the face of a clock and start the TTouch at 6.00. Guide the skin once around the clock and continue on to 9.00. Then slide your fingers lightly to the start of the next circle. The reason why we start at 6.00 (rather than 12.00) is to give the circle the quality of *lift*, rather than dragging the skin *down*. If you ask a friend to try this TTouch on you starting at both places, you will feel the difference. Be sure to anchor your thumb so it maintains a connection to the horse and your fingers. A word of warning: do not *slide* your fingers over the horse's skin, but instead move the skin over muscle.

What you should do if …

• **Your horse doesn't like to be TTouched**
Try lighter or stronger pressures, vary the speed, and apply TTouches on different parts of your horse's body. Make sure your fingers are relaxed and soft, that the circles are really round, and made in one smooth, flowing motion. Watch your breathing – keep it quiet and rhythmical – and stand with your knees "unlocked". If your horse will not stay still for any type of TTouches, do some ground exercises (starting on p.36) to settle him, and get him to listen to you.

• **Your horse shows no reaction**
Not all horses show that they like being TTouched. Find out what your horse enjoys by watching for small signals – a slight drop of the head, change in respiration, or closing of an eye. Even if he doesn't show any signs of pleasure, the TTouch will improve his general health through sensory impulses.

Raccoon TTouch

Named after raccoons, who make tiny movements with their nimble paws when washing their food, this TTouch is a series of tiny circles done with the tips of your fingers (not your fingernails). Hold your hand in the same position as for the Clouded Leopard TTouch, only curve your fingers a little bit more. By increasing circulation to an area the lightness of the Raccoon TTouch is effective for delicate work: treating bruises, and reducing swelling around injuries – even on painful places. It is also useful on body parts where the skin lies directly over the bone – e.g. the eye area or coronary band.

THE LYING LEOPARD TTOUCH

The Lying Leopard is a variation of the Clouded Leopard TTouch where more of each finger makes contact with the horse. Use it on particularly sensitive, "touchy" horses, or ones with nervous dispositions.

Why use it?

The lightly cupped, or almost flattened, hand being laid on a horse's body makes a larger area of warm contact than just the pads of the fingers. Since you use a gentle pressure with the flat of your hand only, it produces a soothing effect that helps a horse relax. The Lying Leopard reduces tension, nervousness, stress, and helps horses get over their resistance to being cinched or girthed. It is gentle enough to use on fresh injuries to help reduce pain and the possibility of swelling. When an area is really painful, very lightly cup your hand over the wounded area and move the skin in a circle with a "two" pressure, keeping the raised, cupped portion of your hand directly over the injury.

Which parts of the body?

LYING LEOPARD TTOUCH

1 It is similar to the Clouded Leopard, the difference being that you flatten the curve of your hand so the areas shaded in this drawing are touching your horse. This allows a larger area of warm contact with your extended fingers and the heel of your hand. Remember to keep the joints of your fingers slightly rounded. Doing so will maintain a softness in your hand, arm and shoulder. Place your other hand somewhere else on the horse's body to help you stay balanced.

2 As with the Clouded Leopard, this TTouch is a single, clockwise circle made with the thumb stabilizing your hand, and your fingers resting on the animal at 6 o'clock (the bottom of the circle). With your fingers push the skin around a circle and a quarter, then pause and release. The circle begins at 6 o'clock so it is initiated with a "lifting" of the skin. If you start at 12 o'clock, the fingers pull down and tighten the skin rather than release it.

3 After completion of each circle, pause briefly and slide over the hair to the next spot for another circle. An average time for completing one circle is two seconds.

What you should do if ...

• Your horse won't stand still and accept this TTouch

Try the circular movement counter clockwise. If this doesn't help, change the speed – make the circles slightly faster, and then slow them down as he relaxes. Or try different pressures. Make sure your circles are round, your fingers soft, and that you are breathing rhythmically. Your state of mind will affect your horse so take a little time to clear your head and breathe deeply before beginning. When you are focused and relaxed, your horse will tend to mirror your state of mind.

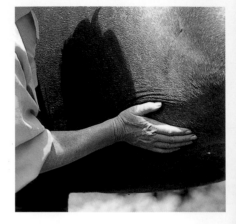

Abalone TTouch

This is a large, flat-handed TTouch that uses the entire hand to conform to the shape of the area being touched. It moves more of the skin in areas such as the girth, belly, or flank. It is also useful on the heavily-muscled body parts – shoulders, back, croup and inside of the thighs. This TTouch helps an animal breathe, or release his breath if he is holding it. It is effective on 'girthy' horses who react badly during saddling.

Remember...

This TTouch is particularly useful on young horses. You can build self-confidence through its contact.

THE PYTHON LIFT

This TTouch is used mostly on a horse's legs to stimulate circulation and improve his stride, and make him less likely to stumble or shy. It can also be used to relieve muscular tension and spasm in the neck, chest, shoulders, and back of the quarters.

Why use it?

The Python Lift reduces spasm on a "girthy" horse, which is often looked upon as the horse being ticklish. Because it improves circulation, it is effective on horses during trips in the trailer, helping them keep their balance, or during breaks on long trail rides.

What you should do if ...

• Your horse doesn't like to be touched on his legs
Stroke the legs from the top, all the way down to the hooves, with the wand. Once your horse accepts this, try some TTouches down the leg, then switch to the Combined TTouch (circle with a Python Lift). Python Lifts from elbow to hoof will calm a spooky or generally nervous horse.

Which parts of the body?

PYTHON LIFT

1 Both hands are placed on either side of the leg (or on the body). Using enough pressure to support the skin and tissue, gently lift slowly upward. Lift only as far as the skin moves easily. Do not force, or feel you are *dragging* the tissue upward. Pause for four seconds and then *slowly* carry it back down again to where you started. You can vary the pressure, the extent of the lift, and the speed, but make sure your hands are not just sliding over the skin. Take twice as long for the downward movement to increase circulation and enhance the relaxing effect.

2 Slide your hands down the leg about two inches, and repeat the lift.

3-4 How you hold your hands depends on whether you are squatting (3), or standing (4). Unless you are sure of your horse, it is safer to stand. If you squat, stay off the heel of your foot so you are well-balanced and can get up quickly if you need to. Organize yourself so you have the largest possible surface area of your hands on your horse.

5 The fetlock joint is the lowest point on the leg where you can do the Python Lift.

Linda's tip

When a horse's flight instinct is triggered, blood is drawn away from his extremities to supply his heart and lungs. By increasing the circulation in the legs you can help to override this flight reflex. The horse will gain self-confidence and be safer to ride. Obviously, you must do the Python Lift carefully in this situation, being ready to move out of the way. It is a very useful TTouch to perform on horses who grow fast and become large when still young. It often takes such horses longer than others to learn how to use their bodies and legs. The Python Lift brings feeling to their legs and they soon learn balance and coordination as they become more grounded and aware of themselves.

The Combined TTouch

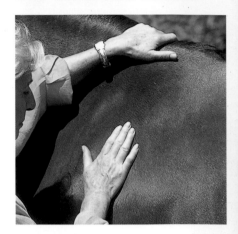

This TTouch is a combination of the Lying Leopard and the Python Lift. Start a circle as usual, and when you come back around to 9 o'clock continue lifting the skin straight up, until you are even with 11 o'clock. Now pause, and then slowly bring the skin straight back down until you are even with 6 o'clock. You can do the Combined TTouch all over the body and I often connect each TTouch with a slide across the hair on the horse's body and start another circle and lift. If you do it on your horse's head, lift the skin up with the pads (not tips) of your fingers instead of your whole hand.

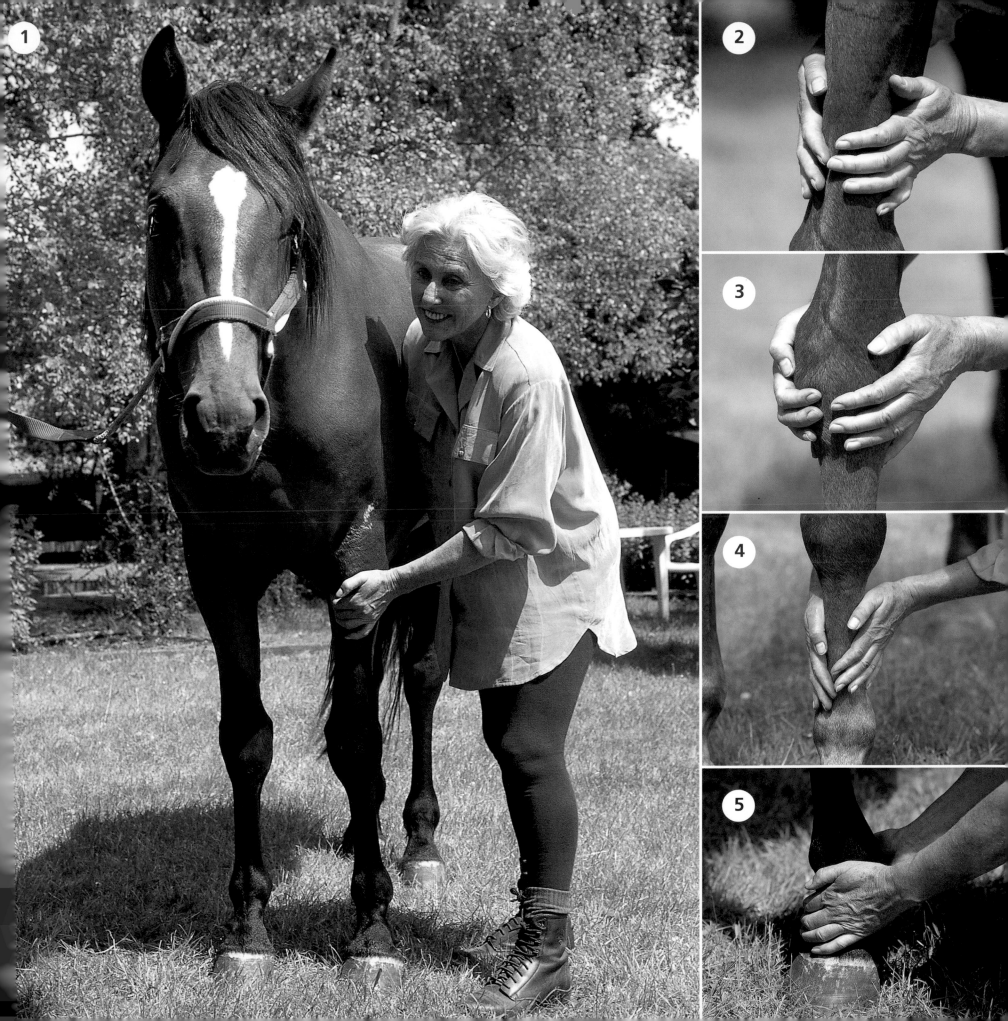

EAR WORK AND TTOUCHES

TTouching the ears affects the whole body of the horse. You can do this to calm a nervous or frightened animal, reinvigorate a tired one, lower pulse and respiration, and alleviate pain and shock caused by an injury or colic.

Why use it?

The effectiveness of working the ear in humans is well known in acupressure and acupuncture. The same is true for horses. Stroking the base of the ear (where the triple heater meridian wraps around) affects the digestive, respiratory, and reproductive systems. For example, when fear overtakes the horse, the respiration becomes elevated, often accompanied by a tight feeling in the stomach. The quickest way to alleviate these symptoms is to stroke the ears. The rest of the ear has many points influencing other parts of the body, and, if stimulated, the immune system can be influenced in a positive way. The beauty of ear work is that you don't need to know where all these points are located. Stroking the entire ear from the base to the tip (where the point for shock is located) can save a horse's life by keeping him out of shock until your vet arrives.

EAR WORK

1 Stand in front of your horse and lower his head with one hand on the side of the noseband, while the other strokes the ear from base to tip.

2 If your horse is sensitive about having his ears touched, do some Lying Leopard or Abalone circles on his forehead. Then move your hand to stroke the base of his ear with the side of your hand.

3 To get the most relaxation in the area around the ear, bring the ear a little forward (see position in photo), and slide your hand from base to tip. Remember to hold the noseband on the opposite side from this ear so you can balance the slight pull with a little resistance, as well as keep the horse's head straight.

4 Once your horse is comfortable having his ears stroked, slide your thumb along the inside of his ear at the same time. This can prepare you to do tiny Raccoon TTouches (page 14) on the insides and outside of his ears. There are acupuncture points throughout the ear which relate to different parts of the body. These points can be stimulated by the TTouch to improve general health, and when dealing with specific organ dysfunction, stiffness, or arthritis. Raccoon TTouches inside the ears help prepare the horse for medication or clipping.

The Llama TTouch

Horses who don't like to be touched on the ears, often accept a TTouch if you use the back of your hand instead. Curve your fingers, and make circles with the back of your hand on the horse's forehead and ears. Some horses don't like to be TTouched anywhere on their bodies. We have found that they often accept Llama TTouches instead. (Note: other ways of making TTouches acceptable to horses who show resistance are to put a woollen sock over your hand, use a sheepskin mitt, hold a small hot pack in your hand, or just wet it.)

Linda's tips
• To calm your horse down on a windy or cold day before your ride, or at a competition where he is nervous and excited, do five minutes of Ear TTouches. You will find this can save you half an hour of warm-up time that you would otherwise need to calm him down. It has an added advantage of loosening up a stiff horse before you even get on.
• When you do the Ear TTouches in an emergency situation, do them fast and firmly.

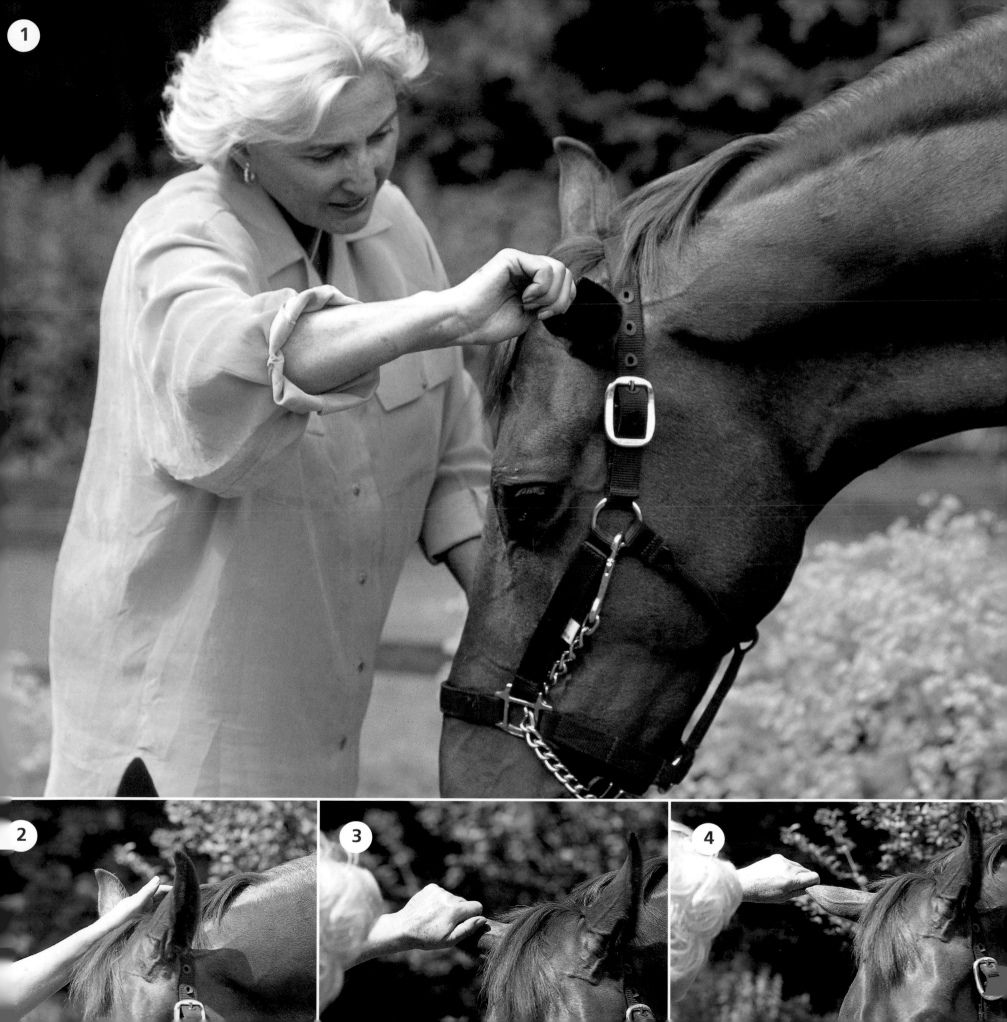

MOUTH WORK AND TTOUCHES

The area under the upper lip is directly connected to the limbic system, the brain's emotional center and the "gateway to learning".
Working on mouth and gums can change attitudes such as stubbornness, flightiness, unwillingness to be caught, etc.

Why use it?

In TTEAM, mouth work is the standard way of dealing with resistance, nervousness, teeth grinding, as well as biting and nipping. It is also an excellent preparation before worming, floating (rasping) teeth, and a good way to prepare young horses to accept the bit.

Remember...

Mouth work is probably a new experience for your horse. If he pulls away, use the chain over his nose to steady his head, and if he throws it up high, fasten the chain up the side of the halter (see photo 4). You want to show him how to lower his head and hold it steady. A horse that is difficult to bridle will often change his attitude about the procedure once he learns to open his mouth from a thumb inserted gently into the corner between his lips.

MOUTH WORK AND TTOUCHES

1 Once your horse has learned to "give" you his head, stand facing the same direction and hold the halter firmly with one hand. Begin with a few Lying Leopard TTouches around his whole mouth, muzzle, and chin area.

2 Slip your fingers between his upper lip and his gums leaving your thumb on the outside of his mouth. If his mouth is dry, wet your hand so it will slide over his gums more easily.

3 Keeping your fingers close together and high up on top of his gums under his upper lip, slide your hand back and forth four or five times. Hold the halter firmly with your other hand.

4 Gently knead the lower lip between your thumb inside the horse's mouth and your fingers hooked behind in the groove of his chin. Start in one corner and work all the way around the lower lip to the opposite corner. With your thumb you can lightly rub all over the inside lower lip or make connected circles. Five minutes of TTouches like this can work wonders with a nervous horse.

Tongue work

Slide two of your fingers into the horse's mouth where the bit normally sits on top of his tongue. Use your middle and index fingers to tap the tongue as if you are playing the flute or piano; rest your thumb in the chin groove. Many horses will open their mouth wide or toss their head because of the strange sensation, but with a little persistence on your part they soon settle and enjoy the contact. Hold your horse's head firmly by the side of the halter and keep your fingers in the natural space between his teeth, known as the bars of the mouth.

The tongue is a strong muscle and could suck your fingers back to the molars. This possibility is minimized by the secure position of your thumb. Tapping on the tongue resensitizes a dull or hard mouth, and a horse with an oversensitive mouth will get used to this contact and learn to respond more willingly to the bit.

What you should do if ...

• Your horse avoids mouth work by lifting his head up
Go with him. Lift up under his jaw and raise his head a little higher than he has. Support it there for thirty seconds or so and then gently allow it to come down. Most horses will maintain a lower head carriage afterwards. If there is still difficulty, return to the head-lowering exercise (p.10) with the chain up the side of the halter. Sometimes you will be more successful if you use the back of your fingers or cover your hand with a damp cotton sock or cloth and make counter clockwise circles all round the outside of his mouth. This usually works wonders on the most defensive horses.

• Your horse nips or bites
With a dangerous biter use Taming the Tiger (page 12) for safe control. But, first practice the Mouth TTouch on a friendly horse until you feel confident doing it. Many young horses nip because they were allowed to "mouth" a human when they were foals. Nipping or biting is also the result of normal playfulness or just plain boredom. Working the mouth while keeping the head still almost always overcomes these bad habits.

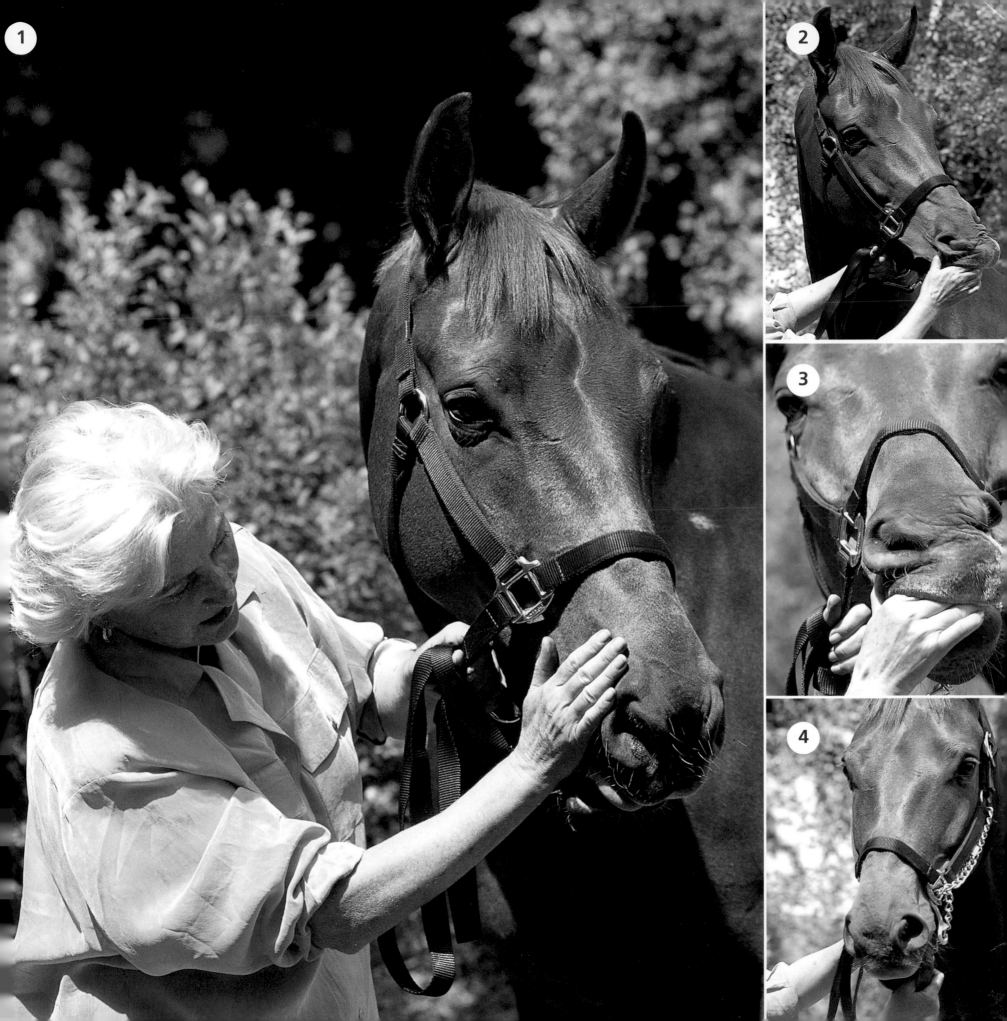

THE BELLY LIFT

Belly Lifts help the horse relax his stomach muscles and breathe more deeply. They can help horses with colic while you wait for the vet to arrive, heavily pregnant mares, stiff or "cold-backed" horses, others who don't like to be girthed (cinched up).

Why use it?

While you are doing a Belly Lift you temporarily override the effects of gravity, relieving tension in the horse's back, which allows his back and stomach muscles to release. In a case of colic you can actually relieve the muscle spasms as well as reactivate peristalsis – the natural motion in the intestines. Most horses take a deep breath and lower their head during this exercise – signs of relaxation – thereby reducing tension or stress.

Remember…

Breathe freely in an even rhythm. Stand with your feet hip-width apart, keeping your knees slightly bent and unlocked. In order to protect your back, keep your weight on the balls of your feet and lift the towel from your pelvis and feet – not just with your arms and back.

Linda's tip

I also recommend you do the series of lifts on young horses as preparation for the saddling process.

BELLY LIFT

1 Take a long bath towel and fold it so that it is about five inches wide. Stand on the left side of your horse and place the towel over his back. One hand draws the lower end of the towel underneath the horse's belly toward you, and the other holds the other end over the top of the back.

2 Keeping your top hand still, very slowly raise the lower end of the towel. Horses usually find this a comfortable experience and stand still. Hold the position for about six seconds. If your horse objects or is nervous about it, hold for a shorter period. And, if your horse obviously enjoys it, you can hold for longer – up to fifteen seconds.

3 Release *very* slowly taking about ten seconds, or roughly twice as long as you held the lift, until the towel is loose. This slow release of pressure is of the utmost importance in producing the desired effect of muscle relaxation.

4 Slide the towel about five inches (one towel width) back toward the flank, lift, hold, and release. Continue until you are as close to the flank as seems comfortable and safe (some animals are very ticklish or sensitive in this area, especially when in pain). You can repeat the sequence of Belly Lifts three or four times, starting each time at the girth and moving backward. In colic cases you will usually hear increased gut sounds during such a session.

Belly Lift with a girth

You can also do Belly Lifts with a girth. Sit the saddle in place and do the lifts as you would with the towel. This is an especially useful exercise for horses who blow out their bellies when being saddled, who object to having the girth or cinch tightened, who are "cold-backed", or have a tendency to buck when first mounted.

Belly Lift with a helper

Belly Lifts can be done by two people, as shown in the picture. One person holds the towel completely still on one side of the horse, and the other lifts with the towel on the other side, pauses for about five seconds, then very slowly releases it.

Having an assistant is very helpful if you do not have a long enough towel to do it on your own.

What you should do if …

• **Your horse is colicky**
First take your horse's pulse and respiration, then call your vet. Next start doing some Ear TTouches (p.20) to reduce his pain before going on to Belly Lifts. Many vets agree that both of these measures are more effective than walking the horse – the standard treatment.

THE BACK LIFT

This TTouch encourages a horse to raise his back by contracting his abdominal muscles. By raising his back the horse will lower his head, lengthen and relax his neck, and release sore or stiff back muscles.

Why do it?

This method of contracting the belly muscles and raising the topline releases the horse's back muscles. As the back comes up, the head usually will go down as the topline lengthens and hollow areas on the back fill in. It is a very good exercise for horses who drop or hollow their back away from the rider, are ewe-necked, sway-backed, stiff, difficult to engage or collect, and who don't step under their bodies with their hind legs.

Remember…

Some horses are ticklish so start this TTouch slowly. If you suddenly press your fingers into your horse's belly it's understandable for him to kick at your hand as he would if a fly landed on his belly. Keep your hand far enough forward so if he does kick at it the first time you ask for a lift, he'll miss you. If your horse is sensitive you may want to prepare him for Back Lifts by first doing some Lying Leopard, Lick of the Cow's Tongue (p.28), or Abalone TTouches on, or around, the midline of his belly.

BACK LIFT

1 Linda is using the wand here to show the difference in height of the horse's back before and after the Back Lift. You don't need a wand for this exercise – it is just being used here for demonstration purposes. When you do the Back Lift, stand next to your horse facing the girth area and start with some Lying Leopard TTouches along the midline of his belly.

2 With your palms up and fingers curved, press your fingertips just beside the midline (see photo on right). You can start out gently and gradually increase the pressure if the animal if not responding, even using your fingernails (medium length, not long.) Do not use constant pressure, but a quick press-and-release motion. Some horses are so sensitive in this area that you can lift their back just using a flat hand.

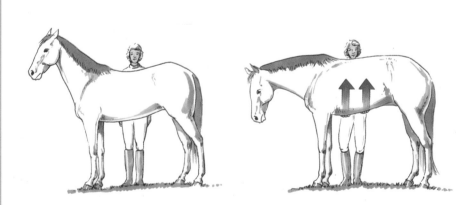

The Back Lift changes the relationship of the vertebrae, which allows the horse to lower his head. This is a very useful, additional effect of this TTouch because all horses, particularly nervous ones, will relax when their heads are down. It's important that you hold the head loosely enough so that the horse can lower it as his back rises.

What you should do if …

• **Your horse doesn't lift his back**

Try using fingernail pressure on different areas next to the midline of the belly. If you are not sure if the horse's topline is lifting, ask a helper to observe for you, because from where you are standing it is not easy to notice the height difference. When your horse responds you can strengthen his back through a regular program of Back Lifts. You may also find eventually that all you need to do is stroke his belly to get him to raise his back.

Linda's tip

To protect your back, stand with your feet hip-width apart, bend your knees, and keep your back straight.

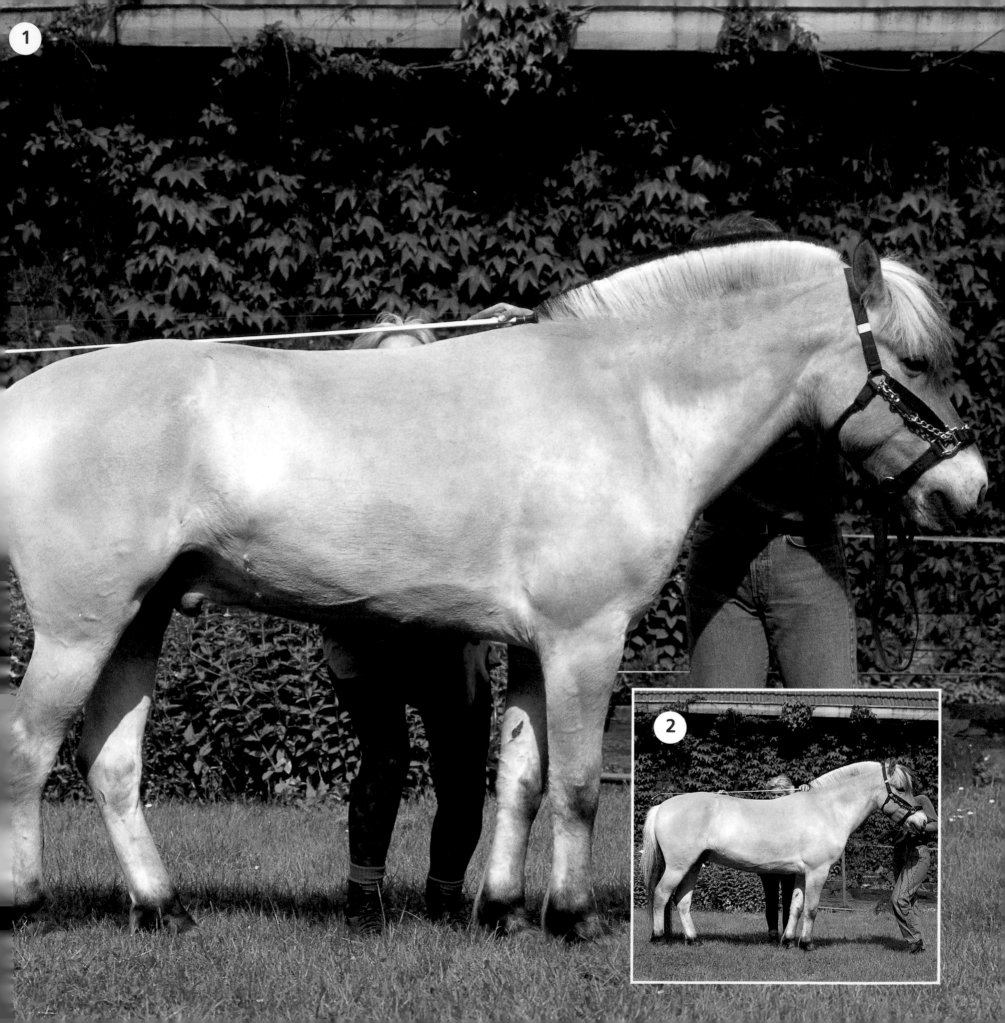

THE LICK OF THE COW'S TONGUE

The Lick of the Cow's Tongue connects horses from belly to back, giving them a better sense of themselves and thereby improving their self-confidence, coordination, balance, and gait.

Why use it?

This TTouch soothes sore, over-worked muscles after a hard workout. It also softens the muscles of horses who are stiff or tight in their back.

Remember…

You will find it improves flexibility, enabling your horse to bend, collect, and perform lateral movements more easily. Just five minutes a day of Lick of the Cow's Tongue even helps very stiff horses happily roll after they have been ridden! You can also do this TTouch on the shoulder, neck, or hindquarters, always going across the hair.

Linda's tip

If your horse is hot and sweating after work, put a damp cotton sock or cloth over your hand while you do the long strokes of this TTouch. The damp sock cools the horse whilst the TTouch helps him recover from his exertion more quickly.

THE LICK OF THE COW'S TONGUE

1 Stand next to the girth area. Place one hand flat on the horse's back, belly, or chest for balance and connection, and start your Lick of the Cow's Tongue TTouch with the other hand in the middle of his belly.

2 With your fingers slightly apart and gently curved, place your hand, fingers pointing away from your body, under the belly just past the midline. Draw your hand toward you across the hair with a long, soft stroke.

3 As you start to come up onto the barrel of the body, rotate your hand so your fingers point upward, just past the midline.

4 Continue across the hair and complete the motion, crossing over the spine. The contact is with the tips of the fingers and the heel of the hand. Start the next TTouch one hand width behind the first one. Try different pressures and speeds, and make sure to work both sides of the horse.

A variation

If your horse is overly sensitive to the long strokes you can combine them with Lying Leopard TTouches. Slide across the skin for a short distance, do one circle TTouch, slide a bit further, do another circle, and continue in this manner until his muscles relax and he is not ticklish any more (see the drawing). This may take several sessions.

What you should do if …

• **Your horse remains ticklish, or his skin twitches**

Try different TTouches altogether. Start with Belly Lifts, Abalone TTouches, then, with a much lighter pressure than before, attempt the combination of Lick of the Cow's Tongue and the Lying Leopard TTouches as described in the variation.

• **Your horse doesn't like to be touched in the udder or sheath area**

Many people do not pay enough attention to the udder and sheath areas, which need to be cleaned like the rest of the horse. If the horse needs to be introduced to being touched there, start with Abalone TTouches using a warm, damp, cotton cloth or glove. Acknowledge any concern that the horse shows by pausing momentarily, letting him know that you are indeed listening to him, thereby gaining his trust.

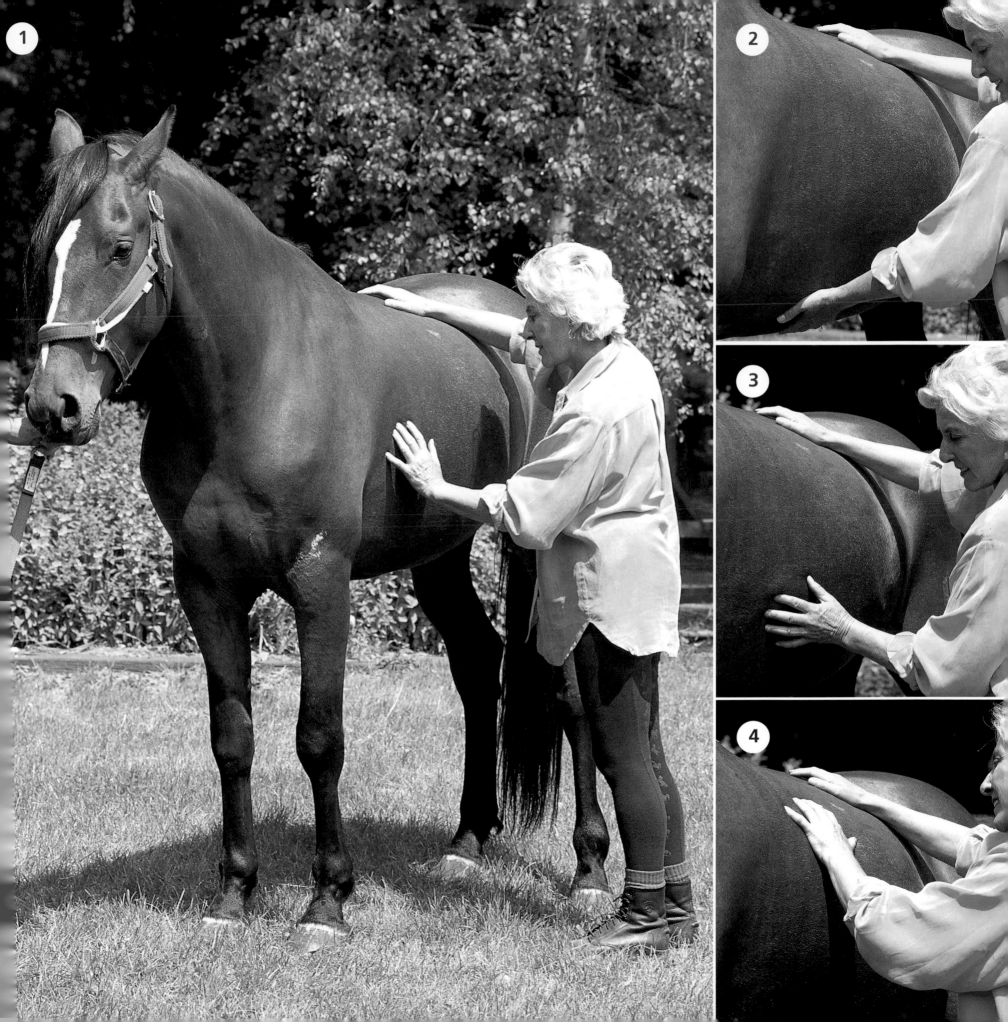

TAIL WORK AND TTOUCHES

Tail work consists of TTouches on, and movements with, a horse's tail. It relaxes the back, and increases the horse's awareness of his hindquarters. This improves balance and gait, stops nervous tail swishing, and prepares horses for breeding, or wearing a crupper.

Why use it?

Tail work helps horses who are afraid of noises or movement around them or at the rear, who kick at other horses, or lash out in the trailer. Frightened horses often tuck their tails in. If you can change this habitual posture you can change the associated fearful behavior. As their tails and hindquarters soften, their confidence and attitude will improve.

Remember...

Only stand behind a horse when you are certain he won't kick. If in doubt, you can do much of the work easily and safely while standing to one side. From this position pick up the tail with one hand by holding a clump of hair on top of the tailbone while the other hand rests on the top of his quarters. Circle the tail in both directions and apply gentle backward traction on the tail. Pause. Slowly release. This will prepare a nervous horse for more tail work.

Before you start, do some circular TTouches – Lying Leopard or Raccoon TTouches – down the buttocks and on the top and to the side of the tailbone to relax the hindquarters. Often the horse will then lift his tail voluntarily.

1 **Tail circling:** Pick up the tail as follows (see drawing on left). Put one hand under the tail about eight inches from the top. Lift the tail. Place the other hand on top of the tailbone about two-thirds of the way down. Push the tail inward with your lower hand as you lift up with your other hand, creating an arch. Circle the tail like a propeller several times in each direction.

2 **Tail pull:** Stand directly behind your horse. Hold one hand about eight inches down the tailbone, and the other hand twelve inches down. Stand in a balanced position, with one foot forward, the other back. Slowly apply traction by shifting your weight over your rear foot, pause for 4 or 5 seconds and very slowly release the traction by shifting your weight forward again. You can repeat two or three times. It is important to do this exercise gently with an awareness of the movement through the horse's spine. Do not use your strength.

3 **Pelvic tilt:** Hold some tail hairs with each hand and place your fists on the point of the horse's seatbones (see the drawing above). With one foot in front of the other, push by shifting your weight forward. Hold the pressure for a few seconds, then slowly release backward. Repeat on the other side.

4 **Tail flex**: Take the tail in both hands so that your fingers are underneath the dock and your thumbs on top. Move every single vertebra gently up and down – not side to side. Start at the top of the tail and move downward. You will notice that closer to the end the vertebrae are fused and less flexible.

Linda's tip

If your horse has a very "loose" tail – when you start to pull and there is little resistance, as though the tail is attached with a loose rubber band – pull very carefully. You can strengthen the connection from tail to body by holding the tail with both hands close to the top and instead of pulling, push the tail toward the spine.

What you should do if ...

• **Your horse has a tendency to kick or won't stand still**
Don't work around the tail until your horse has lost his fear of being touched behind. If your horse will not stand still when you try to do the tail pull or the pelvic tilt, try doing the exercises more slowly and pulling or pushing more gently.

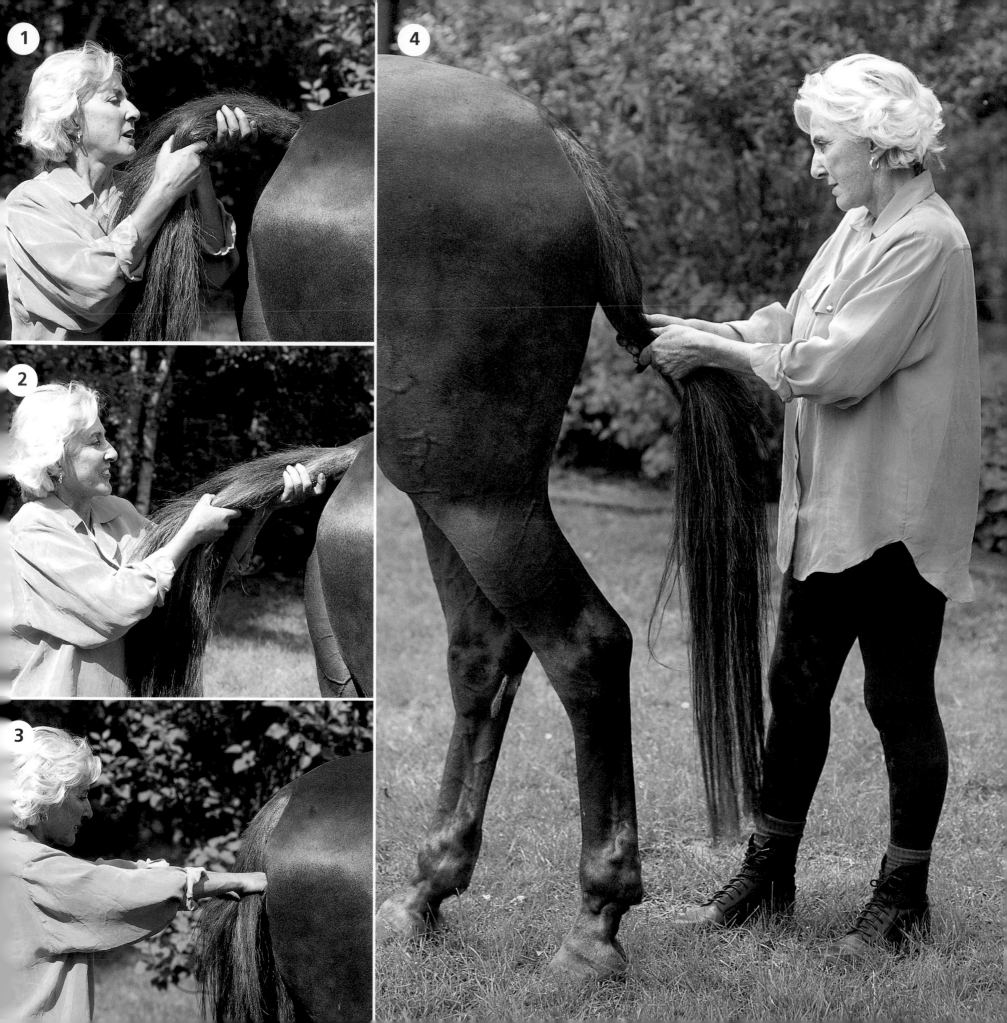

FRONT LEG WORK

In just two minutes a day you can do circle exercises with your horse's front legs to improve his balance and surefootedness, relieve tension in his hindquarters, and lengthen his stride.

Why do it?

These circles relax your horse's shoulder, neck, and back muscles and improve his balance. Consequently, his stride improves, he stumbles less, stops dragging his feet, holds them up more easily and stops leaning on the farrier. As you become familiar with the normal way your horse feels, you will have a way to detect back or leg stiffness before it shows up as lameness under saddle.

Linda's tip

Horses who can't stand still in the trailer or who lean against the side or middle divider for support, have shown that leg work helps them travel much more easily. Their new-found, balance helps them have a safer ride. When you finish a leg exercise (or cleaning out a hoof), avoid dropping the foot – guide it down and place it on the ground.

Remember…

Circle the legs "out of" your pelvis, knees and feet. To avoid strain, keep your back soft and straight, and rest your outside elbow on your outside knee.

FRONT LEG CIRCLES

1 Position yourself facing the hindquarters and prepare to pick up your horse's foot by stroking down the leg with the back of your hand. Then, with your fingertips or fingernails, pinch or squeeze at the back of the leg between the knee and the fetlock. This signal teaches the horse to take his weight onto his other three legs and re-balance to lift his foot. Support the fetlock joint with your inside hand. Your outside hand supports the hoof, your thumb is on the heel, and your fingers are around the front of the hoof. As much as possible, avoid flexing the fetlock joint and keep the sole of the foot perpendicular to the ground.

2 Circle the hoof in both directions around the point where it had initially rested on the ground. Use a horizontal motion like a helicopter propeller: toward the other leg, forward, to the outside, and then back. Do circles in both directions (two to the left, two to the right) at several different heights from the ground, spiralling down until you are just above the ground. Instead of putting the hoof down, do another circle as close to the ground as possible and tap the toe on the ground at several points on the circle. Then place the toe on the ground about six to eight inches behind his other leg so the shoulder releases in a non-habitual way. If your horse is very tight in the shoulder or low in the heels, resting the toe may be difficult at first. With some horses it's necessary to "build up" the ground using a block of wood or pile of leg quilts/wraps for a couple of sessions until they can release to the ground. Stroking the tendon when the toe is down relaxes the leg and shoulder. Most horses rest the toe for only a moment. This position improves balance.

What you should do if …

• **Your horse has a tendency to pull his leg away**

Don't get into a struggle. Remember it takes two to fight. Instead of hanging on for dear life, give the leg a little shake, or vibration. You can also let the horse put his foot down to regain his balance. Then, try again, and this time ask for only one or two small, fast circles before letting the leg down. Do this a few times until he seems more secure standing on three legs. Add some Python TTouches from elbow to hoof to improve his awareness of the area and take away any fear he might have of being handled there.

• **He leans on you when you pick up his leg**

Support the leg at the fetlock joint and under the cannon bone. Fold the leg at the knee, keeping the lower leg parallel to the ground, and raise it high enough so that your horse cannot lean on you. Horses often lose their balance and lean when the handler holds the hoof higher than the knee. Give the leg a little shake to encourage him to be responsible for his own balance. Steady yourself and don't lean into the horse.

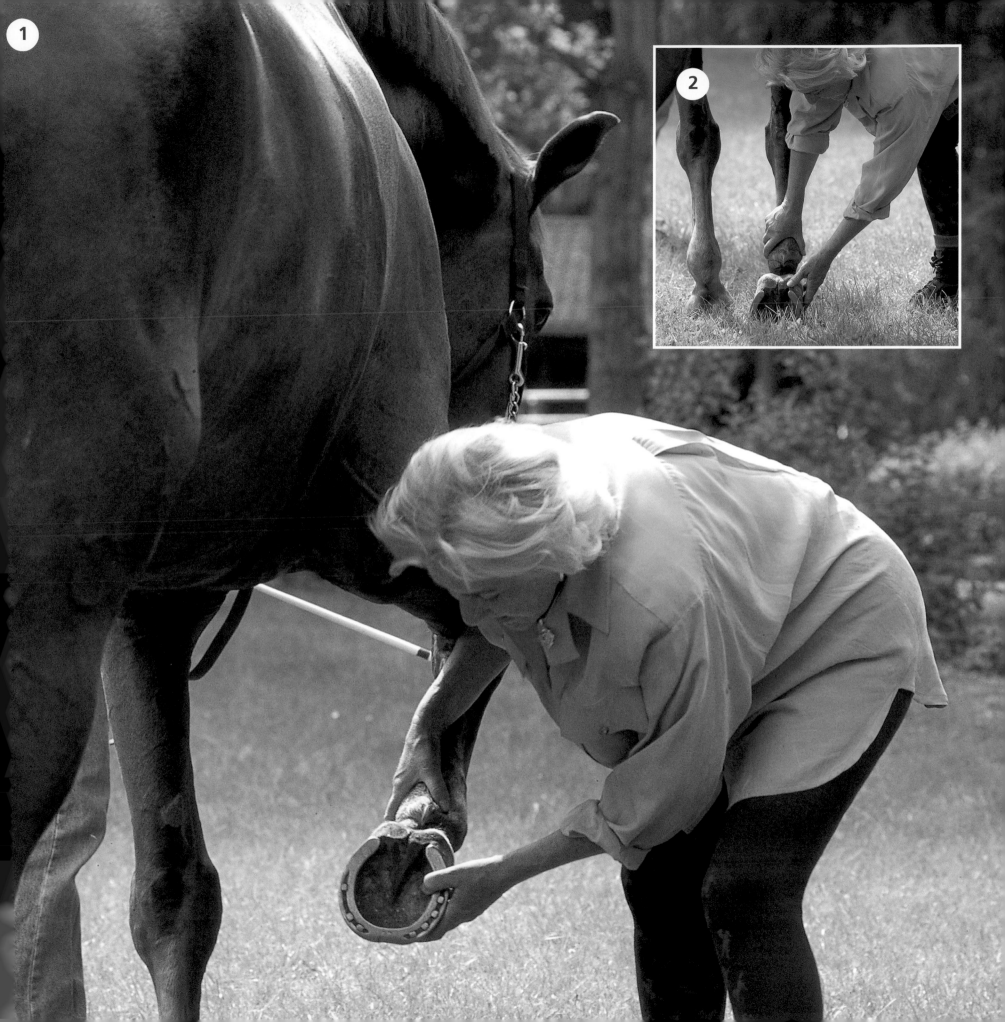

HIND LEG WORK

Manipulating a horse's hind legs in circles is a non-threatening exercise. It has been found to lengthen a horse's stride considerably and increase his ability to move freely with greater suppleness and engagement.

Why do it?

In many cases, hind leg circles have the effect of bringing about an evenness of gait to horses who previously were short and choppy behind. In addition to improving locomotion, a horse's willingness and ability to stand quietly for a farrier are greatly improved. Horses who are a problem for farriers are often out of balance and may be nervous about having their hind feet handled. Therefore, they tense their large hindquarter muscles all the way up into the back.

Remember...

For a horse who is frightened – kicks, threatens, or pulls away – stroke him quietly with the wand used like an extended arm. Start the stroking on the chest and front legs and then proceed along the belly and down the hind legs. This will help him gain confidence about being touched and will improve his balance by "reminding" him of his connection to the ground.

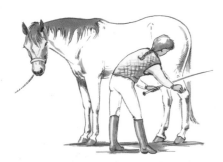

HIND LEG WORK

1 Place your outside hand (right in this picture) on the outside of the hoof with your outside elbow resting on your outside knee. Bring your inside hand around the inside of the horse's leg: use your hand to support the leg around the back, just above the fetlock joint. Start with some circles at the height and in the position offered to you by the horse. As you do with front leg work, use *all* of yourself in making these circles. Try different sized circles: a healthy, athletic horse should be able to manage a sixteen-inch circle comfortably. Circle the leg in both directions at different heights working your way down to the ground. Rest the toe of the hoof six to eight inches behind the other hind foot. This position helps the horse relax all the muscles in his hindquarters.

2 In this picture Linda is still using her right hand to hold the hoof, but is grasping the *front* of the leg just above the fetlock joint. This may allow you to circle the leg more easily, but only works with horses who are balancing well.

3 Leg circles under the belly: draw the hind leg forward with your inside hand on the back of the fetlock joint and your outside hand drawing the hoof forward. Imagine a line between the horse's front and hind leg on the same side. Draw the leg forward and then "draw" an oval, moving the leg under the horse's belly, toward the back, to the outside and then forward again. Do this several times in both directions. Take the leg only as far forward as is comfortable for the horse.

Linda's tip

If your horse cannot balance himself when you attempt to make the hind leg circles larger than six inches in diameter, take heed. It may be a sign that he has a tense, or sore, back. Don't attempt to stretch or force the horse but continue to make just small circles. After a few sessions, the muscles of his hindquarters and his back should relax. When they do, you will be able to gradually make larger circles that will help increase his range of motion and improve his way of going.

What you should do if ...

• **Your horse has trouble performing lateral work (such as side passes/half passes), or flying changes**

Leg circles under the belly teach a horse to move his hind legs freely to the front and side – without the weight of a rider. It will be easier for a horse to do any sort of lateral work as his range of motion increases. The non-habitual circling allows him to become aware of how all the parts of his legs can function, and help him organize different movements, such as flying changes.

• **Your horse will not hold his leg up for long**

Just do one or two fast, small circles, and then let the leg down. If your horse is not a dressage horse (who needs to stop and stand squarely), ask him to rest his toe slightly behind his body. With one hand on his hock, jiggle the leg. This will help relax the hindquarters and make it easier to pick the leg up again. For arthritic horses, or those lame with stifle problems, be conservative and just make small, low circles, i.e. do not pick the leg up too high.

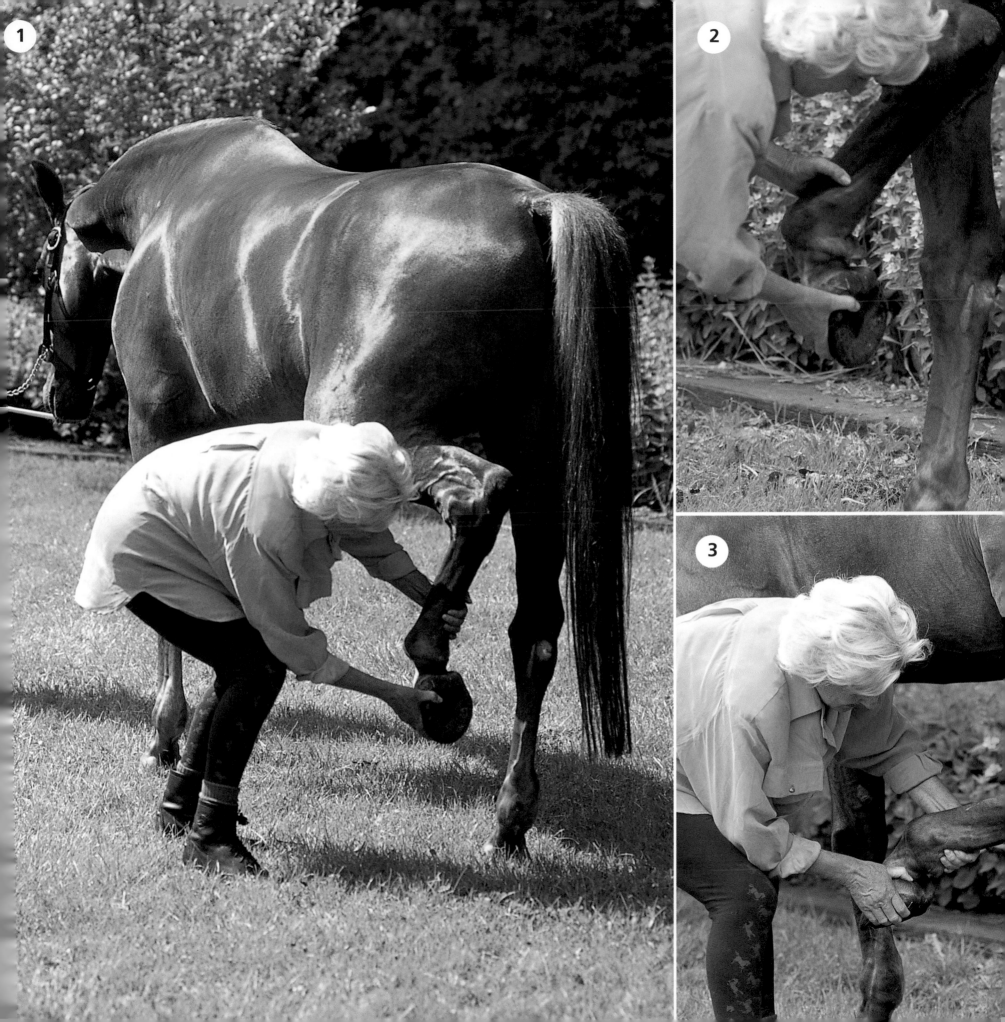

TTEAM GROUND WORK

TTEAM ground work is comprised of two parts: leading exercises and obstacles.

The leading positions

• are non-habitual and therefore encourage a horse to think and learn, in a new, effective manner;

• help a horse to find his own balance without the complication of a rider's weight;

• teach a horse a more effective way of carrying himself by altering his head position, lightening his forehand, and engaging his hindquarters;

• teach a horse to wait for a signal before moving.

GROUND WORK – WHY DO IT?

Most people spend part of their time with their horses leading them from the barn or yard to the pasture, and from the stall or stable to the arena. They take leading for granted, not realizing they have a golden opportunity to teach their horses to be obedient, patient, balanced, coordinated, focused, and in self-control – all qualities that carry over to riding. The TTEAM leading exercises greatly encourage a horse's willingness to cooperate, as well as improve physical coordination and confidence of both horse and rider. At TTEAM we have many different leading positions – and as with the TTouches, we have given them animal names – Elegant Elephant and Dancing Cobra, for instance – because we have found that not only do people remember them easily, but they add an element of humor to the training process and humor engages our brain in a way that enhances our ability to learn.

Obstacles such as the Labyrinth, the Star, working with poles and plastic sheets, are another integral aspect of the TTEAM ground work. The obstacle exercises teach the horse to use his body in a way that improves balance, self-control, precision, fine motor skills and eye/hoof coordination. Because the way he has to move in the obstacles is non-habitual it helps him to differentiate this movement as well as give him a feeling of connective wholeness throughout the body. By asking your horse to move in a non-habitual pattern – for instance in the Labyrinth to take one step and stop, two steps and stop, do the half-walk, bend around the corners – you can alter his coordination and balance, and develop a willingness to cooperate. Another non-habitual movement is asked for in the Star, where the horse's legs on one side have to be picked up higher than those on the other side.

At TTEAM we believe that every time we handle a horse we are teaching a lesson – be it positive or otherwise. Since most of us have limited time to spend working with our animals, it seems sensible to make each time a positive experience – deepening the understanding and partnership between horse and rider.

The obstacles

• improve a horse's confidence as he successfully negotiates a new challenge;

• give a horse an awareness of how his body moves by encouraging him to think about what he is doing;

• teach the handler to be clear with his signals and reinforce how light a signal can be if your signal makes the intent clear;

• teach a horse to concentrate and wait for the handler's signals;

• keep the handler in constant communication with the horse;

• are designed so that they can be made easier if the horse has difficulties.

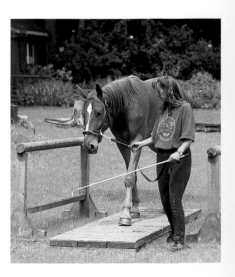

Leading tips

• Remember to release tension on the chain after giving the signal. You may have to signal and release more than once before a complete "whoa" is achieved. If you pull or tug continually on the chain, the horse will pull on you, or move around you in a circle.

• Allow for a delay while the horse processes your signal, and organizes himself to do what you are asking.

• Use clear intention to draw a "stop" line with the wand two feet in front of the horse, followed by a tap or two on his chest, rather than just flapping it up and down in front of his face.

• Staying in front and to the side of the horse's nose, instead of back by his shoulder, gives you more control. In this position the horse can see you and more clearly understand, and respond to, your cues.

• Keep your hands soft.

• If the horse keeps getting in front of you and won't stop, slide up to the Elegant Elephant position (p.40) and stop him. Do not just yank on the chain and circle the

horse around you – it just pulls him off balance and speeds up his actions. You want your horse to stop and stand as straight as you expect him to under saddle.

• Practice leading the horse from his right side. It's also non-habitual for both horse and handler (and you may feel incredibly awkward the first time you try it) but it teaches the horse balance, and how to bend to the right.

• When asking the horse to stop, keep a low "whooaaaa" tone until the horse actually fully stops. By developing a toning pitch with your voice, the horse's brain-wave patterns are affected, which in turn helps in the learning process.

• For all positions, with the exception of the Glide of the Eagle, the end of the lead is in your left hand when you are on your horse's left, and vice versa. Remembering this will make it easier when you switch sides.

• The most effective learning is not through repetition. Once the horse has demonstrated he knows something, stop the exercise. Nothing is gained by repeating it until he makes a mistake.

Safety tips

• Always wear sturdy shoes and, if you are working with a young or difficult horse, wear gloves, too.

• Work in a fenced-in area where your horse will concentrate – not in a grass-filled pasture full of temptation!

• No extra points are won by surviving a dangerous encounter. TTEAM methods such as the Homing Pigeon, and Taming the Tiger, provide ways of dealing with horses safely.

THE BODY WRAP AND ROPE

The body wrap and body rope are TTEAM training tools that ease anxiety, increase awareness, and improve your horse's performance by giving him a better sense of how he uses his body.

Why use them?

A strung-out horse can quickly discover a more balanced stance, and his topline may change so he looks "rounder". During ground work, the wrap and rope can reassure horses who shy at objects, and help those who are stiff, or who rush or are lazy. (The apparent contradiction in being able to change both laziness and rushing is answered by the explanation that the wrap and rope help the horse to come into balance regardless of how the imbalance is expressed.) They also encourage horses who "freeze" (often called stubborn), and give horses the confidence they need to stand quietly for the vet or farrier. Finally, they help horses cope with challenges such as entering confined spaces – trailers or narrow doorways.

Linda's tip

Using the body rope on a foal is an excellent way to teach him to lead and stand quietly. It keeps the foal in balance and gives you control of his body without pulling on his head. Always practise with the foal's dam along and keep your lessons short. You can hold the twist at the withers as if it was a suitcase handle, and give signals by moving it backward or forward.

1 Body wrap: The body wrap consists of two elastic bandages secured together. Wrap one bandage around the horse's neck and tie it with a knot. Attach one end of the second bandage to this knot, then gently guide it around the horse's hindquarters (always watching your horse's reaction) and tie the other end to the first bandage about fifteen inches away from the first knot. As you see in the photograph, pull the first bandage while attaching the second so the bandages sit just behind the withers and just below the point of the buttock. The idea is to form a "bridge" of wrap, going over the horse's back just behind the withers. Make sure the second bandage fits snugly and does not slide down the horse's back legs when he walks.

2 Body rope: The body rope is a length of rope about twenty-three feet made of strong, soft nylon that is tied in a figure of eight around a horse's body. The rope touches and moves away from the horse as he steps. Twist the rope at the withers (see photo) and tie with a bow or quick-release knot as shown. Ensure that the bow or knot is in the handler's reach and that the dangling rope ends do not irritate the horse. The back of the rope should hang about eight inches above the hocks.

Riding with the body wrap and rope

When riding, run one wrap, or the rope, behind the horse and attach the ends to the billet (girth) straps of your saddle. Before mounting, walk and trot the horse in hand to familiarize him to the sensation. Riding with a wrap benefits horses who shy, are afraid of things behind them, or who drop their backs. Riding with the rope is best suited to horses who swish their tail, who do not use their hindquarters well, or who drag their toes, kick, and who are stiff through their bodies.

Remember...

Prepare your horse for the sensation of the back part of the body rope by guiding it gently around his hindquarters without tying it to the front part. Hold it in place over the horse's tail and walk a few steps with a helper leading your horse. Once he has accepted the feel, you can tighten the rope a bit. Later, when your horse shows no apprehension at all, place the rope under the tail, and tie it with a quick-release knot or bow as in photo 2.

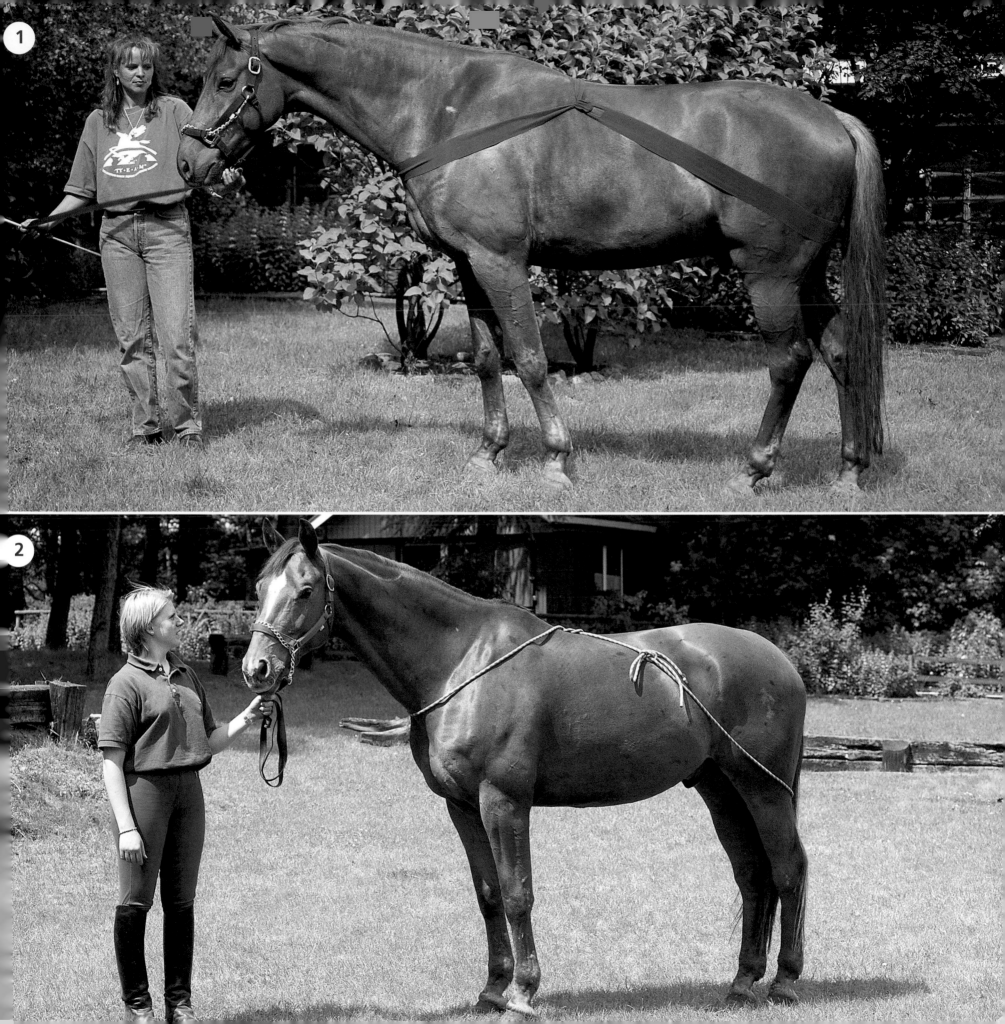

THE ELEGANT ELEPHANT

The Elegant Elephant is the most basic, and most secure leading position used in TTEAM. It is useful for every horse who offers any problems to his handler, and is also the easiest leading position to learn.

Why use it?

The Elegant Elephant is an excellent leading position for a horse who has a tendency to pull, is heavy in the hand, difficult to stop, or circles round the handler. The horse will be easier to control because the handler is ahead of the horse and can keep him straight. When the button end of the wand is carried so the horse can see it, it gives him more information about what the handler wants. Remember the horse responds to clear, rather than forceful, instructions by exhibiting greater patience, relaxation, and cooperation.

Remember...

Placing the extra loop of the lead line between your index and middle finger enables you to quickly shorten or lengthen the lead line if your horse moves or jumps quickly. Doing this avoids the risk of having the line wrap itself around your hand or fingers.

THE ELEGANT ELEPHANT

1 Basic position: When leading your horse from the left, stand just ahead of his head and hold the lead line in both hands with your right hand on the chain portion. Tie a knot at the end of the lead and place it across the palm with the knot near the little finger. Take up the slack of the lead line in a loop between your middle and index finger (see photo). Also with your left hand, hold the wand midway down its length, with the knob in front of the horse.

2 To invite the horse to walk forward, move the wand slowly, directing the button end of it forward along the path you intend your horse to follow. Use your right hand to give the forward signal and release on the lead line, and use your voice "and waaaaalk". Think of your right hand as if you were using it to turn a key in a lock.

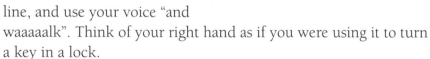

3-4 To stop, stay even with your horse's head, not at his shoulder. Give the voice command – a long, soft, drawn out "whoaaaa". Hold the tone until your horse stops. (This also encourages you to breathe deeply.) Holding the wand about twenty inches from the horse's face, move it slowly up and down about three or four inches in the area between his eyes and nose. With the button, tap the horse's chest once or twice on the opposite shoulder from where you are standing, while you give him the signal to stop with the chain section of the lead line – a light tug backward, and release.

What you should do if ...

• **The horse turns towards you as soon as you ask him to halt**
Be sure to stay in front of your horse (by his head) and keep moving until your horse has stopped. Hold the chain section of the lead line very close to the halter and keep his head straight. Don't forget to touch your horse's outside shoulder with the wand.

Linda's tip

To practice handling the lead line and the wand efficiently, do it without the horse. Tie the lead line to a fence, and while standing parallel to the fence pretending it is your horse, practice the light tug-and-release signal to go forward and stop. Remember that the horse will act on the release part of the signal rather than on the tug.

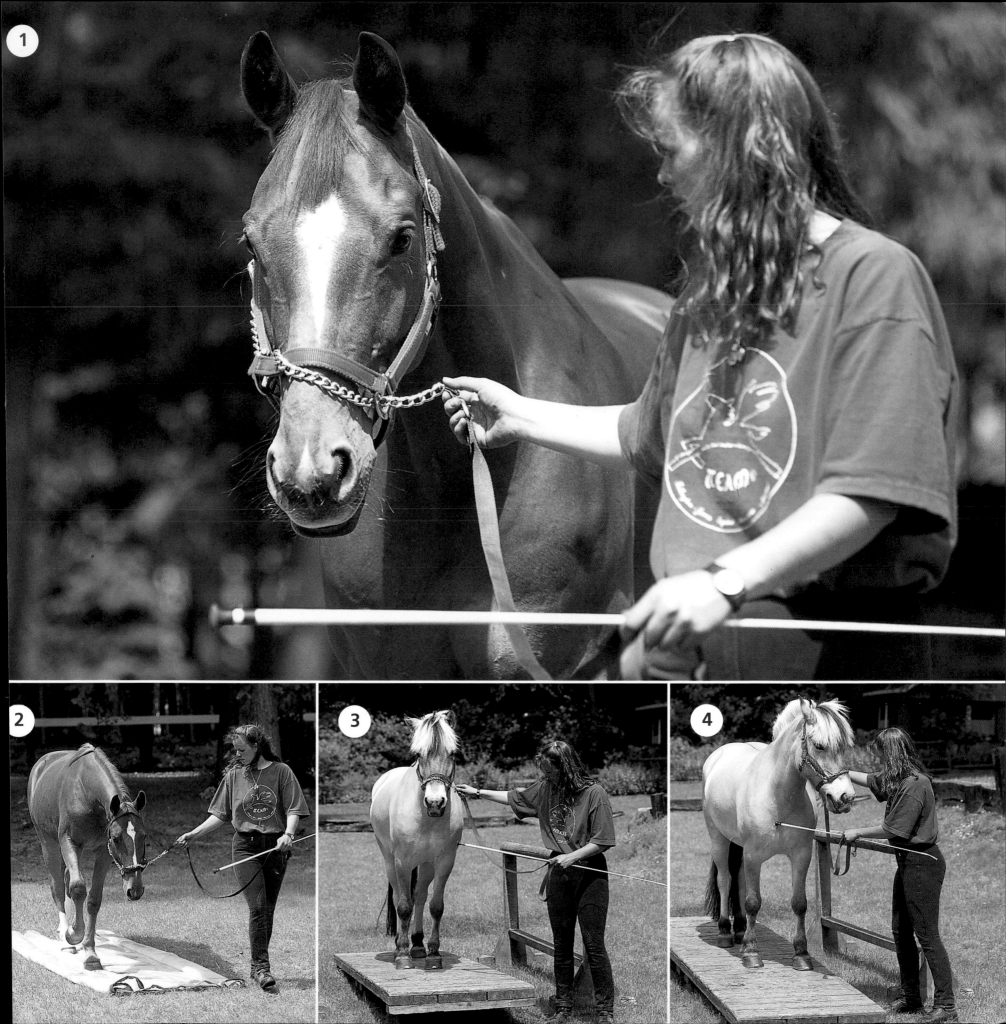

THE DINGO AND CUEING THE CAMEL

These two leading positions help teach your horse patience and obedience. They also give you the possibility of being able to influence his posture and how he uses himself.

Why use them?

The horse learns to respond to clear, precise signals both at his head and on his body, which will carry over to work under saddle. The action of the wand can be used when mounted to clarify "go" and "whoa". Slow horses learn to respond faster, and impatient horses learn to wait. The exercise also greatly helps your horse's frame; he can learn to carry himself and engage his hindquarters. The Dingo is excellent for teaching a young horse to lead, a timid horse to walk forward, and any horse to load into a trailer.

Linda's tip

The goal is to teach your horse to react to the slightest signal. If you find you have to keep tapping your horse to make him move forward, make sure you are not causing the reluctance by holding him back with your hand on the lead line. It takes time for most people to use their hands independently, so practicing this ground exercise will help you with your riding.

THE DINGO AND CUEING THE CAMEL

1-2 The Dingo: Note that the lead line is held in one hand only and is looped safely. This exercise has four steps: steady, stroke, signal, and scoop. Steadying your horse with a light contact on the chain, stroke his back gently with the wand two or three times from the withers to the croup.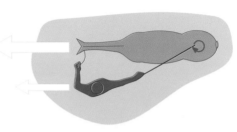
Then give a light, forward signal and release on his halter, and a *forward-scooping* tap, tap, tap with the wand on the top of his croup. At the same time give the verbal command, "and waaalk".

3 Cueing the Camel is usually used in conjunction with the Dingo leading position to stop your horse. Bring the wand to the front of his chest pointing the soft end of it down toward the ground as you move it forward. Signal your horse to stop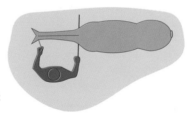
with a long, drawn-out "whoooaaa" as you give a light signal on the chain and tap him on the chest. The tapping encourages him to shift his weight back and stop in better balance.

The Platform

When taking a horse over an obstacle like the platform (see photos) or the Bridge (p.58), use the Dingo leading position. These obstacle tests are excellent exercises to build your horse's trust in going where you ask him, even if it seems threatening. In particular, they prepare your horse to learn to be loaded into a trailer without any fuss and apprehension.

What you should do if ...

• **Your horse falls onto his forehand as he stops**
Lift the chain up, and slightly backward, to help re-balance him.

• **Your horse is nervous**
With the lead line, ask him to lower his head below the withers (see p.10). Gently tap his croup with the wand and move forward with his head low. Practice walking forward for just two steps, then stop. Give light and clear cues – with the wand on the chest and the lead line. Remember to use clear voice signals for walking forward as well as stopping, to avoid confusing him and adding to his discomfort. An additional tip: this is an excellent exercise to practice with a horse who has a tendency to pull back when tied up (often used in conjunction with Taming the Tiger).

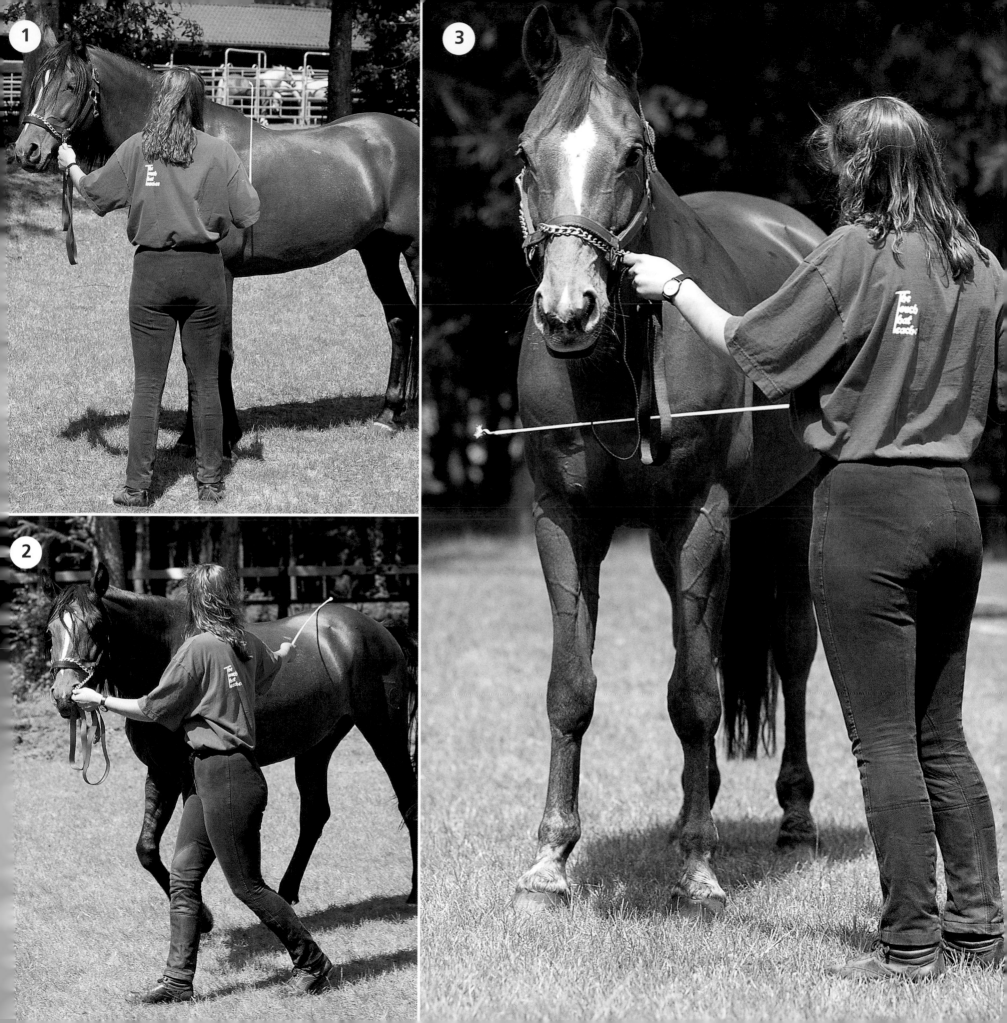

THE GRACE OF THE CHEETAH AND THE HALF CHEETAH

The Grace of the Cheetah leading position teaches your horse to move and respond to signals while at a distance from you, and stop from the wand and voice signals only. This encourages self-control and self-carriage.

Why use them?

Your horse learns self-control and to think for himself. He also gets used to you being further away from him and becomes responsible for his own balance without your help. Insecure horses who like humans close by for reassurance become more confident.

Linda's tip

If you have an anxious horse – one that pulls you forward – the Grace of the Cheetah position can teach him to slow down without yanking on his head. The importance of having his head free is that pressure on it can increase his anxiety. To keep him back, just lightly tap his chest with the wand. If this doesn't work, switch to the Half Cheetah and combine all three signals – voice, wand, and lead line.

THE GRACE OF THE CHEETAH AND THE HALF CHEETAH

1 **The Grace of the Cheetah**: Stay ahead of your horse and to one side of his path. Working on the horse's left side, hold the wand at the button end together with the end of the lead line, in your left hand. Your right hand should also hold the lead line about half way up – three or four feet from the horse's head. Hold the line lightly, and put your thumb on top (see photo). Use the wand movements plus your voice to indicate your wishes.

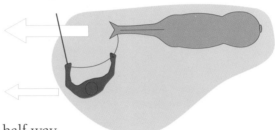

2 **The Half Cheetah**: Your body and hand positions are the same as for the Grace of the Cheetah, but you are closer to the horse, and your leading hand is closer to the halter. Use this position for a horse who is difficult to hold back – it gives you the opportunity to signal with the lead, which is not recommended when you are further away from the horse. You can reinforce the lead and voice signals by touching the outside shoulder with the wand.

Leading your horse into water

One of the great benefits of these leading positions is that your horse learns to follow the wand into places and terrain that may frighten him. His increased self-control and confidence makes him more trusting and obedient.

Remember...

The wand used in TTEAM work has proven very useful. It is stiff and sits well balanced in your hand, so you can use it with great precision. It is also white, so your horse can see it easily. When using the chain lead line, make sure that the chain part coming off the halter is no longer than four or five inches. When the chain is too long its weight can pull the horse toward you, or swing around too much when the horse is trotting.

What you should do if ...

• **Your horse is afraid of the wand**

Get him used to the wand by stroking him all over his body. Start with the short, button end toward the horse, and stroke on the under side of his neck and chest. These areas are usually less threatening to horses. It won't take your horse long to lose his fear and accept the wand.

JOURNEY OF THE HOMING PIGEON

The Homing Pigeon leading position 'activates' both sides of the horse's brain, increasing his focus and concentration. It also helps the handler: when she is dealing with a boisterous horse, she can concentrate on the task at hand while her helper keeps her safe.

What do you need?

- One lead line with a chain, and one lead line with a rope.

- Two wands.

Why use it?

The Journey of the Homing Pigeon keeps a horse from leaning on or crowding you. It is useful for horses who pull or are difficult to control, it speeds learning by influencing the horse from both sides, and it helps horses who are one-sided, or reluctant to be led from the right side.

Remember...

The idea behind this leading position is to teach your horse self-control – to respond more to the wand and less to the lead line. The benefits to this is a horse more manageable on the ground as well as lighter in hand when being ridden. Make sure your signals are mostly from the wand only, and are light and precise.

JOURNEY OF THE HOMING PIGEON

1 There are two different ways to do this – both with two people, two lead lines and two wands. Either way, it is important to designate the leader who will be in charge from the very beginning. The leader's chain lead line is fastened in the usual way – over the noseband and up the opposite side – and she may use the Elegant Elephant leading position for extra control. The support person's soft lead rope (no chain necessary) loops through onto the side ring of the halter nearest her and is twisted back on itself, and she stays in the Grace of the Cheetah leading position.

2 Second method: With one person still in charge, both people employ the Grace of the Cheetah leading position so that the horse is influenced by voice and wands only. Both wands are held at the level of his nose, well out in front, which helps the horse to focus on where he is going. To walk forward, the leader gives the voice signal, and both people "open" their wands in front of the horse.

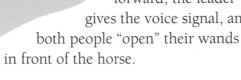

Leading from both sides

This is how you should attach the two lead lines to the horse's halter. Only use two chain lead lines when a horse is a dangerous puller or aggressive. If you do, make sure the chains cross over the noseband, and keep checking to make sure they do not tighten up.

Linda's tip

Both handlers should be far enough ahead of the horse so that they can see each other in front of the horse's nose.

What you should do if ...

- **Your horse rears when asked to go forward**
As soon as he does this, release the pressure on the lead line. When you ask him to move forward again, make sure you keep the wands low, and quiet. The handler may choose to move to the Dingo leading position.

- **Your horse is stiff on one side, and consequently not willing to go straight forward**
This problem can often be solved by taking him along a line of cones (road markers) encouraging him to bend through them, over cavaletti, around the Star, or through the Labyrinth (pages 54 and 56).

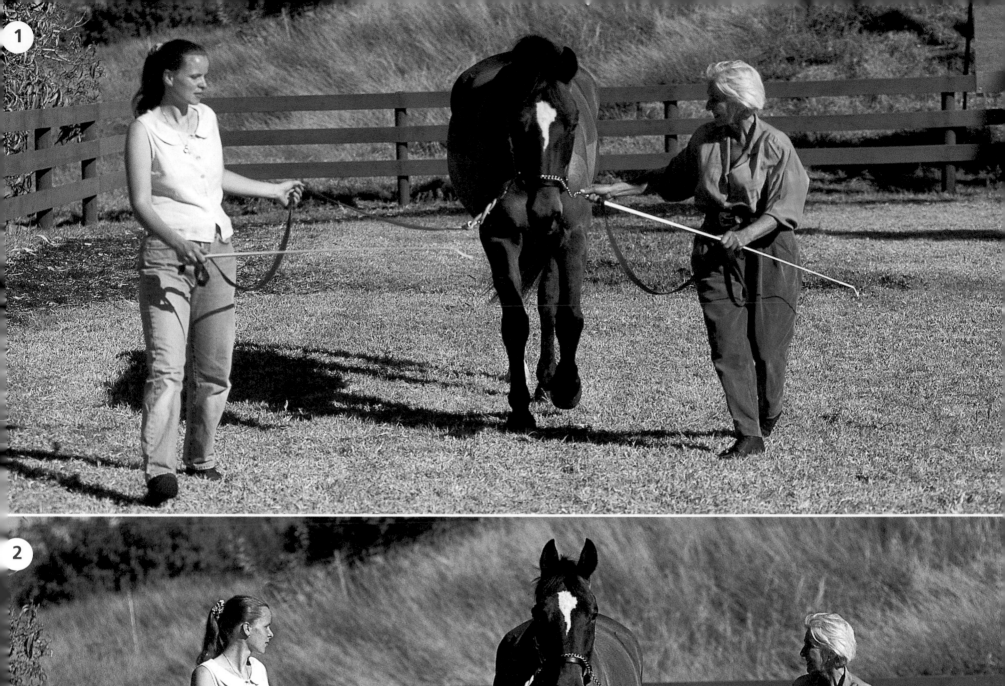

Boomer's Bound And The Peacock

Boomer's Bound is especially helpful when dealing with head-shy horses and young ones who are uncertain about movements above or beside their head and neck (such as mounting and loading). The Peacock position teaches horses to keep their distance.

Why use them?

Both exercises help overcome fear of movement over and around a horse's head and neck. In addition to alleviating the problems associated with general head-shyness and trailer loading, it is a wonderful exercise to use with a young horse who might well get spooked when you first mount. It also prepares him for the unusual or sudden movements on his back when he is first ridden.

Linda's tip

If your horse does not like to have his ears touched, attach the lead line to the side of the halter. Move the wand slowly above his head while giving him a little feed in a shallow container at his chest level. Talk to him quietly while you gently stroke his ears with the wand.

BOOMER'S BOUND AND THE PEACOCK

1-2 **Boomer's Bound**: This is a position to stop your horse after leading him forward with the Dingo. Assuming you are on the left side, stand close to him holding the chain part of the lead line with the rest of it folded in your left hand, while holding the wand in your right hand, close to the button. Move the wand in a large

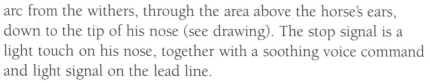

arc from the withers, through the area above the horse's ears, down to the tip of his nose (see drawing). The stop signal is a light touch on his nose, together with a soothing voice command and light signal on the lead line.

3 **The Peacock**: Hold your horse with your right hand, and use your left hand in the middle of the wand with the button end up to move it like a windshield wiper between you and the horse slowly and rhythmically. This exercise teaches your horse to keep his distance from you, and is great preparation for the leading positions Grace of the Cheetah and Dolphin Flickering Through the Waves.

Preparation for loading

Many horses that are difficult to load are terrified by the roof of the trailer so close to their head. One way to encourage them to become more trusting is to ask them to lower their head while moving the wand above.

Remember...

When you work around horses, your feet should always be about hip-width apart, and your knees should be bent slightly rather than locked into a straight position. You should always be able to move quickly in any direction. Practice breathing slowly, as the way you breathe may be mimicked by your horse.

What you should do if ...

• **Your horse is scared by the wand above his head, so he throws his head up and pulls back**

Attach the chain lead to the side of the halter and ask your horse to lower his head (p.10). Use the button end of the wand to make TTouch circles on his head and neck. Lead him through the Labyrinth (p.54) with his head still low, and move the wand slowly above his head.

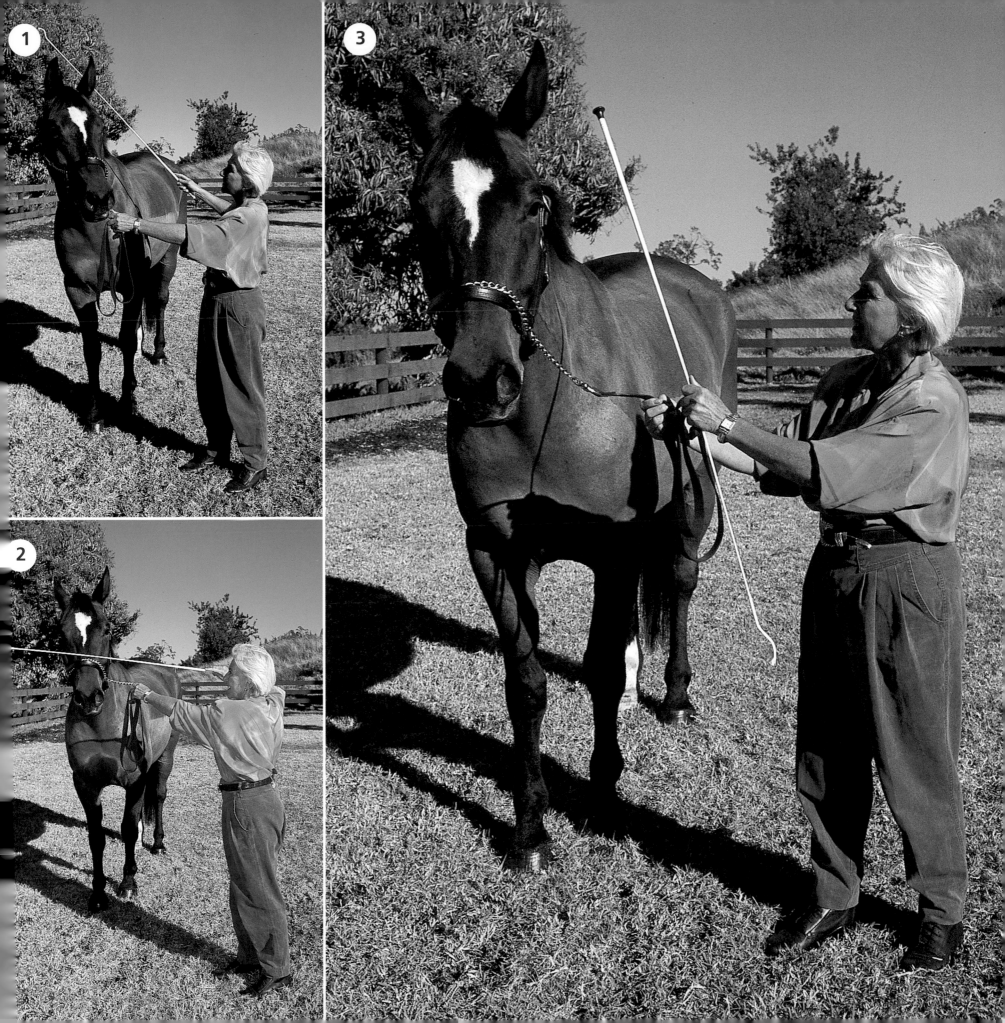

DOLPHIN FLICKERING THROUGH THE WAVES

In this leading position, the tip of your wand jumps softly from point to point over the horse (like a dolphin leaping), from the croup to the withers to the poll to the nose. It teaches your horse to listen to you, and to maintain his distance.

Why use it?

The Dolphin prepares a horse for lungeing, where the horse is at a distance from the handler and also controlled by the voice and a lunge whip. It also gets the horse used to movements above him (from the wand) while he himself is moving.

Remember...

The whereabouts of your body in relation to your horse's position is important for safety reasons. In the Dolphin, always stay level with your horse's shoulder. If you allow yourself to get further behind, the horse will be able to kick you.

What you should do if ...

• **Your horse is crowding you**
It is important to keep the chain short enough so it can't swing and give an unintentional signal to the horse. Use the Peacock (page 48), moving the wand like a windshield wiper between you and the horse to keep a clear boundary. You can tap his nose or neck to ask him to move him away. If he still does not understand, use the Homing Pigeon to give him a clearer idea about keeping his distance.

DOLPHIN FLICKERING THROUGH THE WAVES

1-4 Start with the Dingo leading position. While standing on the left, hold the lead line in your left hand, and the wand at the button end in your right. As your horse steps forward move away from him, out from his shoulder, allowing the lead line to lengthen. Then, give your horse a flick on top of the croup with the tip of the wand, next on the shoulder, then a light tap on the top of the neck and finish with a soft flick on the side of the nose as if you were using a paint brush.

To stop, change to the Grace of the Cheetah by moving into your left hand along with the end of the lead line, and slide your right hand up the lead line closer towards your horse's head. Make a short motion with the wand about three feet ahead of your horse and then tap him lightly on the chest, as you say "whoaa".

Linda's tip

In TTEAM ground work we lunge horses slightly differently from other traditional methods. The main difference is that we lunge on an oval rather than a circle. Also we use a regular lead line and wand so the handler walks with the horse, rather than standing still in the middle of a circle. This helps the horse to keep his balance more easily, and makes him mindful all the time of his distance from the handler and where he is going.

The Glide of the Eagle

Once your horse has learned the Dolphin leading position, hold the lead line with the wand in the same hand. Point the wand toward the shoulder. This will enable you to get as far away from your horse as possible and is most useful for an exercise such as trotting over cavaletti.

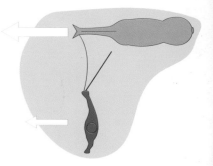

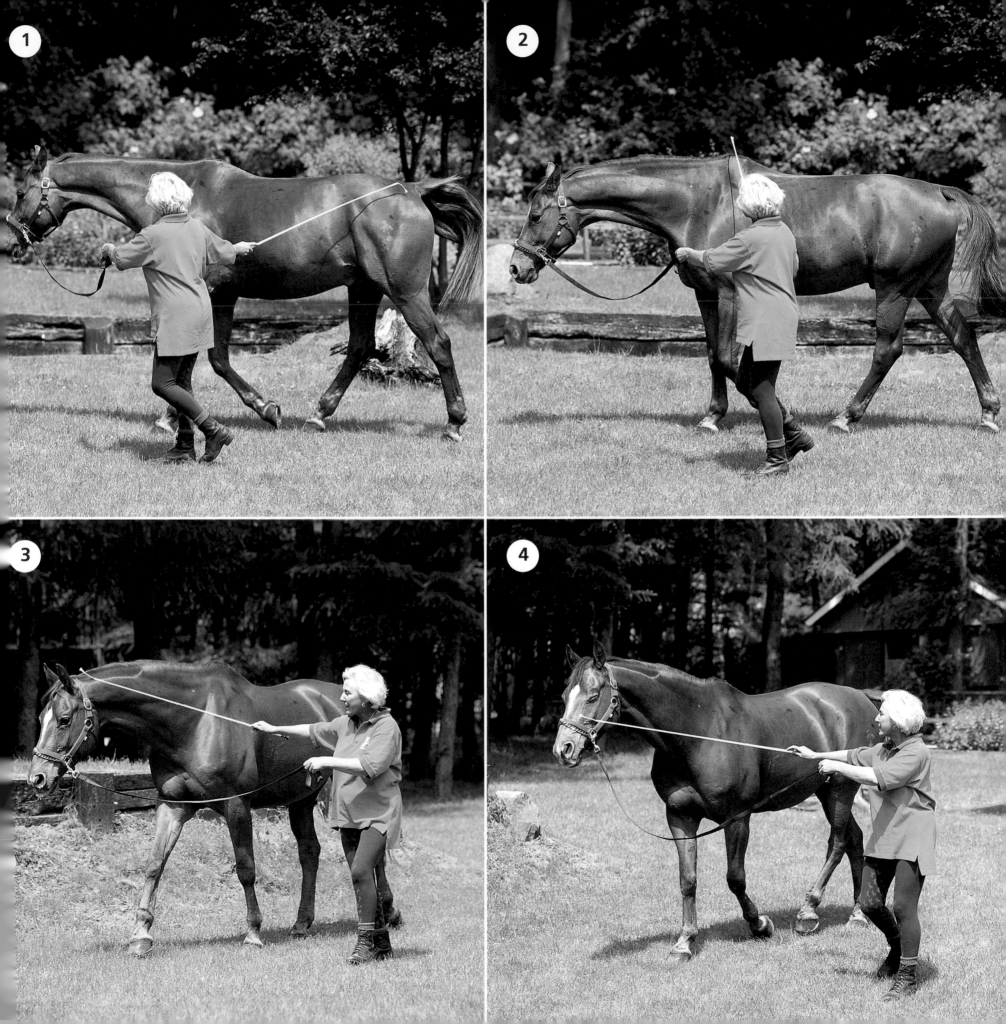

THE DANCING COBRA

This leading position teaches balance, self-control, obedience, focus, and response to aids. The horse learns to stop and stand in balance, patiently without any pressure on the halter, and then step forward as you give the signals.

Why use it?

This leading position teaches a horse to wait for a signal, consequently it is excellent to use on horses who rush at the walk, are pushy and barge their handlers when being led, have poor self-control, or pull back when tied. Instead of pulling back when he feels the tension on the line, he steps forward.

Linda's tip

Practice this position in the Labyrinth (p.54) by first asking the horse to take just one step forward, and stop. Then try two steps forward, and stop. Remember to keep stepping backward when asking the horse to stop (keeping a consistent distance); otherwise as the horse gets closer to you the signals from the wand become unclear.

THE DANCING COBRA

1 **Horse standing still**: stand about three feet in front of your horse and face him, with your body bent slightly toward him to keep him from moving forward. Hold the lead line loosely between both hands: if you've attached the lead to the left side of the halter, hold the end of it in your left hand, and the middle in your right hand. Hold the wand in your left hand and point it toward the horse's nose.

2 **Horse walking forward and stopping**: To ask the horse to come forward, step back with one foot, straighten up, while signaling to the horse with the wand by bringing it across your chest, toward your right shoulder. At the same time give a slight signal-and-release motion on the lead. Ask for one or two steps, then stop him by pointing the wand toward the bridge of his nose and bend slightly toward him. If he doesn't stop, lightly touching him on the nose and chest will bring his head up and help him to halt.

Free work

Once you have mastered the Dancing Cobra with a lead line, try doing it with the horse loose – in a fenced-in area. Start in the Labyrinth with just a piece of string round your horse's neck and using the wand and your body language as emphasis, indicate how you want him to respond. Once he is listening well, you can remove the string and try the exercise with him completely free. Now you can have some fun!

Remember...

If you are working with a stallion and standing in front of him, never tap him on the chest with the wand since this can trigger his fight instinct. Tap him on the nose, instead.

What you should do if ...

• **Your horse won't stop**
Here are three solutions:
(1) Tap the chain of the lead line with the wand. This will cause your horse to raise his head and shift his center of balance further back, making it easier for him to halt.
(2) Review the Cueing the Camel leading position with him so he is reminded of the connection between tapping his chest and stopping.
(3) Get a helper and have her attach a second lead line on the other side of the halter to reinforce your wand and voice signal.

THE LABYRINTH

Taking a horse through the Labyrinth in a guided, specific manner – using various leading positions already described – will promote patience, obedience, correct balance, self-control, and focus both horse and handler on the advantages of being precise.

What do you need?

The Labyrinth is built with six sturdy rails, each twelve feet long. Start by spacing the poles four feet apart. If your horse has a problem getting round the turns move the poles further apart.

Linda's tip

You can make big changes in your horse's balance by asking him to walk one or two steps and stop in the corners as well as in the straight sections. If your horse is difficult to lead outside, put a Labyrinth between the stable and his paddock or field, and lead him through on the way. Horses who move around a lot when being handled will often stand quietly in the Labyrinth. Remember that repetition is not necessary in TTEAM work, so if he does the exercise properly, let him rest and think about it, rather than repeating it until he makes a mistake.

GOING THROUGH THE LABYRINTH

1 All leading positions can be used in the Labyrinth. When you lead your horse through the first time, use the Elegant Elephant, and stop before each turn. Lead from the left side, with your left hand holding the wand and the end of the lead and your right hand on the chain. Hold the wand with the button end in front of the horse. To take your first steps inside the maze, move the wand two to three feet ahead of your horse's nose to create a visual invitation, followed by a light signal and release with the lead to come forward. To halt make a soft up-and-down motion with the wand ahead of the horse where he can see it. Bring it to the opposite point of the shoulder while simultaneously giving a light signal back with the chain. As soon as your horse stops, softly stroke the underside of his neck with the wand.

2 Notice how your horse organizes himself around the turns. Most horses have a "good" side and they can turn in one direction more easily than the other. Start the Labyrinth so his first turn is on his good side, and help him turn in the more difficult direction by leading him from his other side. You may also use the Dingo position and touch him on the croup, thigh, and hock to help him step under himself.

Stepping over the rails

As another exercise, you can use the Labyrinth as ground poles and walk your horse across them. If your horse is reluctant to walk across them, double the distance between the rails.

Remember…

Leave enough space for your horse; do not get in his way. If this means you have to walk in another section of the Labyrinth, or outside it, that is fine. The important thing is that he has enough room.

What you should do if …

• **Your horse trips over the pole while rounding the turn**
Do one, or all, of the following: give him more space by enlarging the Labyrinth. Help him to step forward into the turn by using the Dingo. Raise his head if he appears to be falling forward, or inward, while turning.

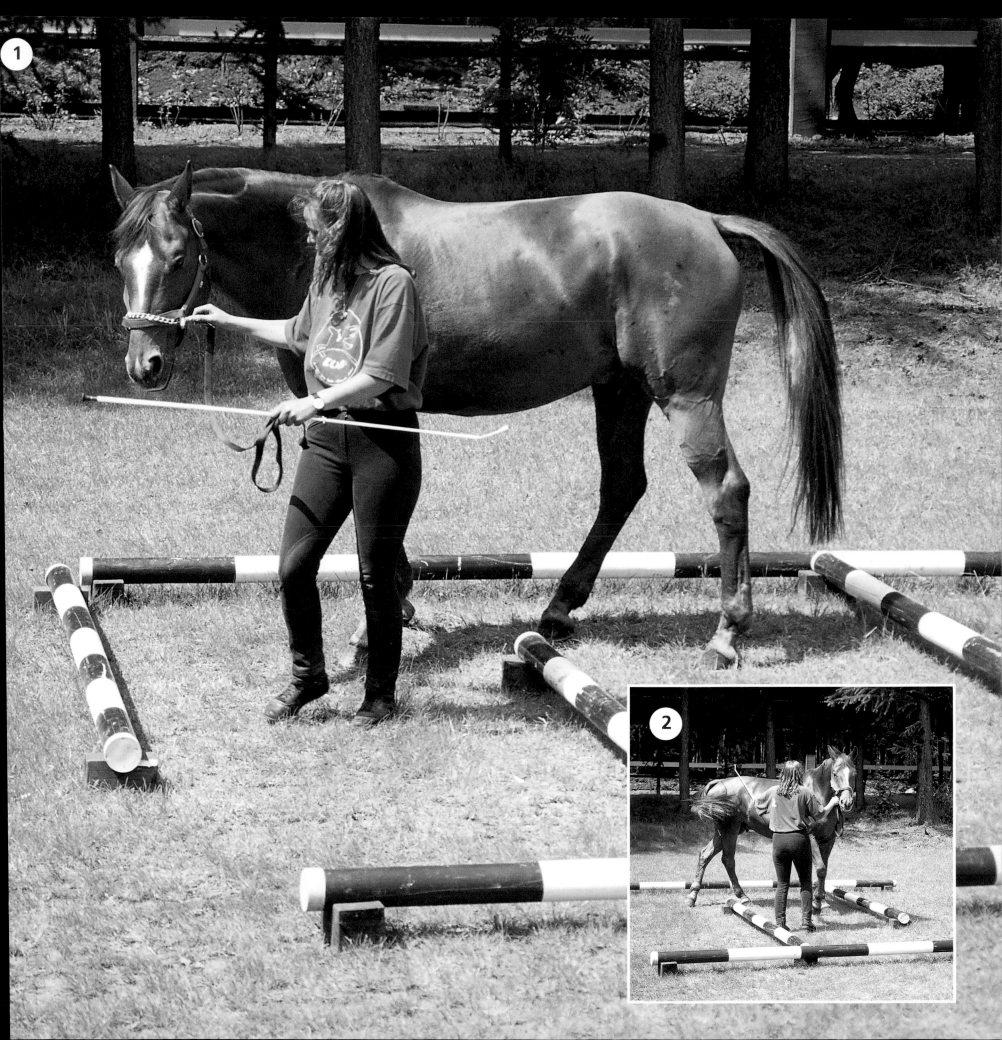

THE STAR, CAVALETTI AND PICK-UP STICKS

Work in the fan configuration we call the Star, over cavaletti, as well as over Pick-up Sticks, benefits horses who are tight in their back, who have trouble bending or stumble, and improves hoof-eye coordination.

What you need

The Star: Four twelve-foot long heavy rails, and an object such as a hay or straw bale, fence, small jump, or tires (tyres) to place poles on.
Cavaletti: four to six, laid out two and a half to four and a half feet apart, six to twelve inches high.
Pick-up Sticks: four solid poles.

Why use them?

Nervous and tense horses gain confidence by stepping successfully over rails. Consequently, they relax. Walking over the uneven rails in the Star improves a horse's hoof-eye coordination, improving his ability to judge height and distance. His flexibility is also enhanced by the exercise – when he steps around the Star the poles are higher on one side of his body and he has to bend at the same time.

Remember…

You must adjust the distance between, and the height of, the rails in relation to your horse's size, gaits, and flexibility. Always start with the easiest configuration – in the Star, start with the poles on the ground about four feet apart at the wide end.

THE STAR AND CAVALETTI

1 **The Star**: To begin, lead your horse over the rails at their lowest point using the Grace of the Cheetah. Make sure you yourself are walking on the high side of the poles – higher than your horse. Walk two rails ahead of him giving him enough room to judge the height and width and adjust his balance on his own. Once this becomes easy, repeat the exercise by going deeper in the Star where he will have to step higher; and challenge him even more by moving the rails closer together, or making them uneven heights. Make sure to lead him from both sides and in both directions. Progress to leading him through in the Dolphin Flickering Through the Waves and Flight of the Eagle positions.

2-3 **Cavaletti**: The advantages of working your horse over cavaletti is that you have a variety of options with the rail positions. You can vary the distance and number of rails, and adjust the height. If you use poles they can be higher at one end than the other. You can lead the horse over the cavaletti, or you can walk beside him while he goes over them on his own. The exercise helps to free a horse's shoulders, hips, neck, and back.

Pick-up Sticks

One way to set up this obstacle is to lay the poles down like a slightly organized "mess" of sticks. You can lay them out to create different-sized spaces for the horse to step into. Be sure they are not set too high, and cannot roll over if they get knocked. Start with the Elegant Elephant, and once your horse is concentrating, switch to the Grace of the Cheetah so he has enough room to lower his head and choose where to place his feet.

Linda's tip

If your horse has a tendency to hit the poles, trip, or shows fear of them, use the wand firmly to stroke his legs right from the top down to the hooves where you tap them with either end of the wand. This should increase his awareness of his legs. Exaggerating your own movement may encourage your horse to mimic you. Lift your legs higher when stepping over the rails, and your horse will probably increase his effort.

What you should do if …

• **Your horse swings his hindquarters out of the Star**
Try these solutions: Lead your horse so that he is on the inner side of the Star, and you are on the outside (wide end). Use a body wrap or rope while doing the exercise. Reduce the number of poles.

Use a rope, or ropes, on the ground instead of the rails.

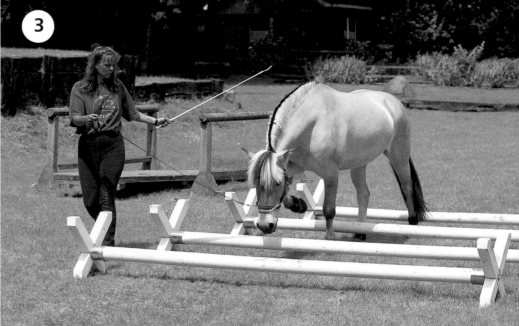

THE BRIDGE, TEETER-TOTTER (SEE-SAW), AND PLATFORM

The hollow sound of stepping on the wood, as well as the boards "giving" slightly underfoot, provide a new experience for your horse. These experiences, as well as balancing on a moving surface, are excellent preparation for trailer loading and travel.

What you need

Platform: Four foot by eight foot sheet of plywood, three-quarter inch thick; or strong boards strengthened as needed.
Teeter-totter (see-saw): As platform, plus a four-foot rail underneath in the center.
Bridge: As platform, with two jump wings on either side.

Why use them?

A nervous horse is often uncertain about stepping onto a surface he feels is not quite solid. Once you have encouraged him, and all goes well, his trust in you will grow. Getting rid of one of his insecurities in this fashion greatly benefits your daily routine.

THE BRIDGE AND TEETER-TOTTER (SEE-SAW)

1 **The Bridge**: A small bridge like this one in the photo is best crossed by using the Dingo leading position. Start ahead of your horse then step onto the bridge, tapping his croup to ask him to come forward.

2-4 **The Teeter-Totter (See-Saw):** Once your horse is comfortable walking over a platform on the ground, you can progress to the teeter-totter (see-saw). The best leading positions to use are the Dingo, or the Elegant Elephant. After the horse has come on to the teeter-totter, ask him to wait for a moment before stepping forward. He may be startled when the obstacle tips downward for the first time, so be prepared. When he is familiar with the object, you can ask him to stop right in the middle and have him rock back and forth by just shifting his balance.

Going over the platform

Work on a large platform on the ground is one of the best preparations for trailer loading and unloading. Start by just walking across the board, then progress to walking the length of it. If your horse tends to drift off the platform, place two rails along the sides to help him stay straight. A horse that is difficult to unload – either refusing to back out, or rushing out too quickly, has often never learned to back up in hand. Teach him to do this on the ground first, then to back off the platform. A good exercise for this is what we call the Dance: using the Dingo and Cueing the Camel, bring the horse forward one step, then back one step by tapping the wand on his front legs (the forward front leg first) and using a light chain action in a backwards motion on the halter. Repeat the step forward and step back.

Linda's tip

If your horse simply refuses to step onto the platform or the bridge, place a little feed on the wood. The chewing will help him breathe and relax, and he will also lower his head. After he takes another step, stop and feed him again. You may also find the Dingo will encourage him to step forward. (When a horse is afraid – of these exercises, or any others – the use of food is an excellent idea. When a horse eats, the parasympathetic nervous system is activated, and this overrides the sympathetic nervous system which instigates the flight reaction.)

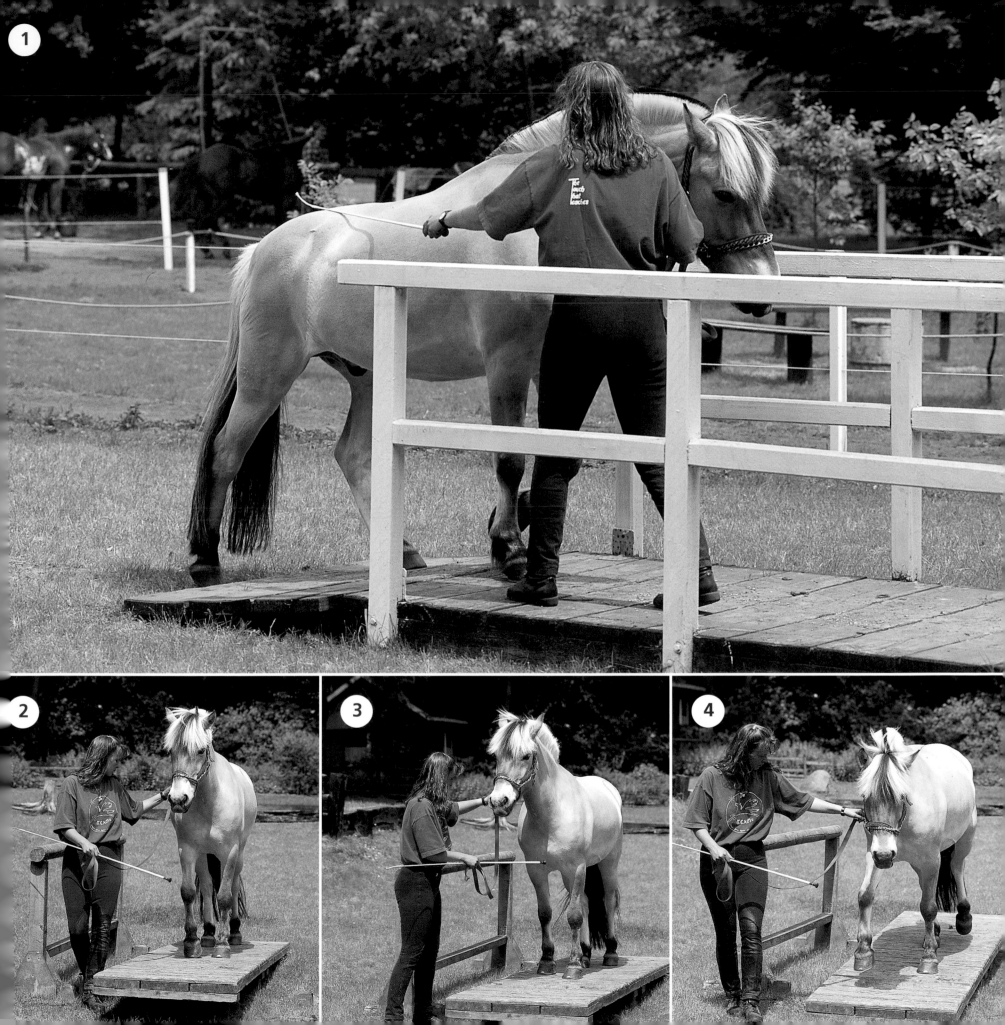

WORKING WITH PLASTIC SHEETS

This is excellent preparation for riding outside on trails (hacking) and at horse shows where "foreign" objects, unfamiliar noises, and flapping tents or flags, appear.

What you need

Two or three twelve feet by six feet sheets of strong plastic. Fold it into two when laying it on the ground to make it thicker for walking on.

Why do it?

This is one of the most important TTEAM exercises to help a horse override his flight instinct and think for himself instead. He will learn to overcome his fear of noisy, moving things; items above him, like you on his back or the roof of a trailer; trash such as plastic bags caught in trees. He will become confident about going through narrow spaces, and stepping on something unusual, even unpredictable, that made him uncertain and afraid before. Like the other obstacle exercises, this one builds great trust between horse and handler.

Remember...

Once your horse is really comfortable with plastic, you can do three exercises together: walk over, under, and through an aisle of plastic at the same time. This is great preparation for trailer loading.

WORKING WITH PLASTIC SHEETS

1 Lay two pieces of plastic quite far apart on the ground in an open-ended "V". Lead your horse up, let him have a close look at both pieces, then lead him through the gap. Give him a bite of food if necessary.

2 Once your horse walks through this gap full of confidence, move the plastic pieces closer together. Your goal is to have him quietly walk on, and over, the plastic at the "V" end.

3 Hang the sheets of plastic over two rails making an aisle and walk the horse through. You can just walk him on the ground, or on the platform as in the photo. If your horse is worried, move the rails with the plastic further apart.

4-5 The last step is to ask your horse to go underneath some plastic. Have two helpers stand on boxes or chairs and hold the plastic sheet in the air. If your horse rushes through at first, make sure you stay ahead of him, give him a loose line, and don't try to hold him back. He will be quieter the next time after he has realized he had no reason to be concerned.

Water on the plastic

If your horse has become comfortable walking on plastic, but is afraid of walking through water, add some water to the plastic sheet on the ground and incorporate this new obstacle into your ground work program. Many horses are frightened of water and this is a most useful exercise to get them used to it.

Linda's tip

When your horse is really too afraid and won't go under the plastic at all, have the helpers hold up two wands. Once used to these, start again with the plastic but have it held really high. You can gradually lower it as the horse becomes more trusting. Some horses get so used to it they will drop their head to go underneath as the plastic slides along their back!

What you should do if ...

• **Your horse is even too frightened to walk under two wands**

Have the helpers hold the wands straight up in the air, and give your horse some feed or a treat in a shallow pan in front of him, or have another handler do this. Use the Boomer's Bound leading position.

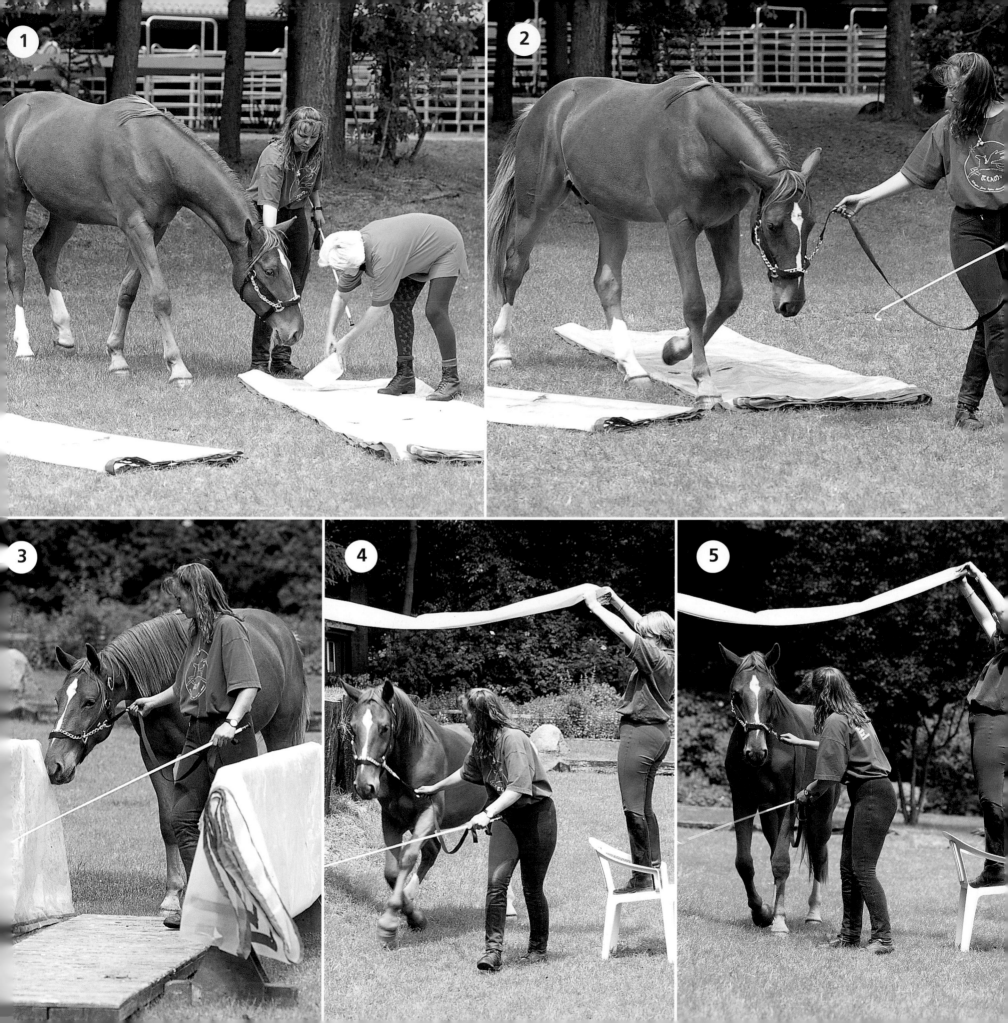

TTEAM ADDRESSES, BOOKS AND VIDEOS

TTEAM Addresses

TTEAM Headquarters
TTEAM and TTouch Training
Linda Tellington-Jones
PO Box 3793
Santa Fe
NM 87501
USA
Phone: 1-505-455-2945
          1-800-854-TEAM
Fax: 1-505-455-7233
e-mail: TTEAM@compuserve.com

TTEAM–Canada
Robyn Hood
5435 Rochdell Rd
Vernon, BC, V1B 3E8
Phone: 1-250-545-2336
          1-800-255-2336
Fax:1-250-545-9116
e-mail: rhood@junction.net

TTEAM–UK
Sarah Fisher
South Hill House
Radford
Bath
BA3 1QQ
Phone: 01761-471182
Fax: 01761-472982
e-mail: sarahfisher@msn.com

TTEAM–Germany
Bibi Degn
Hassel 4
D-57589 Pracht
Phone: 02682-8886
Fax: 02682-6683
e-mail: bibi@tteam.de

TTEAM–Switzerland
Doris-Sueess-Schroettle
Mascot-Ausbildungszentrum
CH-8566 Neuwilen
Phone: 071-6991825
Fax: 071-6991827
e-mail: mascot@swissonline.ch

TTEAM–Austria
Ruth and Martin Lasser
Anningerstr. 18
A-2353 Guntramsdorf
Phone: 02236-47000
Fax: 02236-47070
e-mail: lasser-cbs.tteam@aon.at

TTEAM–Netherlands
Nelleke Deen
Staverenstraat 10 B
NL-3043 RS Rotterdam
Phone & Fax: 01041-52594
e-mail: nelleke@dest.demon.nl

Books

Let's Ride with Linda Tellington-Jones
Linda Tellington-Jones and Andrea Pabel
    Trafalgar Square Publishing, USA, 1997
    Kenilworth Press, UK, 1997

Getting in TTouch: Understand and Influence Your Horse's Personality
Linda Tellington-Jones with Sybil Taylor
    Trafalgar Square Publishing, USA, 1995
    Kenilworth Press, UK, 1995 under the title *Getting in Touch with Horses*

The Tellington-TTouch: A Breakthrough Technique to Train and Care for your Favorite Animal
Linda Tellington-Jones with Sybil Taylor
    Viking Penguin, USA, 1992
    Cloudcraft Books, UK, 1995

Videos

The TTouch of Magic for Horses
The TTouch of Magic for Cats
The TTouch of Magic for Dogs
Haltering Your Foal
Handling Mares and Stallions
Learning Exercises Part 1
Learning Exercises Part 2
Riding With Awareness
Starting a Young Horse
TTouch for Dressage
Tellington-Touch for Happier, Healthier Dogs
Tellington-Touch for Happier, Healthier Cats

TTeam Instructors And Practitioners

For USA, Canada, UK and Australia

USA

Trainer

Linda Tellington-Jones, Santa Fe, NM,
1-505-455-2945

Instructors

Carol Lang, Santa Fe, NM, 1-505-455-2945
Debra Potts, Newberg, OR, 1-503-538-8637

Practitioner 3

Marcy Baer, East Fairfield, VT, 1-802-827-6635
Jodi Frediani, Santa Cruz, CA, 1-831-426-1697
Tina Hutton, Santa Rosa, CA, 1-707-578-3472
Ellie Jensen, Loxahatchee, FL, 1-561-753-5907
Patty Merrill, Ashland, NH, 1-603-968-4455

Practitioner 2

Carol Ames, Leesburg, VA, 1-540-338-5776
Joyce Anderson, White Post, VA,
1-800-447-1787
Pam Beets, Littleton, CO, 1-303-798-6171
Peggy Cummings, Houston, ID,
1-208-788-0797
Judee Curcio-Wolfe, Boring, OR,
1-503-668-5117
Janice Fron, Santa Fe, NM, 1-505-455-2945
Marla Gibson, Terrebonne, OR,
1-541-923-0325
Marie Hoffman, Kirkland, IL, 1-815-522-6230
Julie Jene, Spokane, WA, 1-509-924-9739
Raian Kaiser, Loveland, CO, 1-970-203-0725
Marie Livesy, Legget, CA, 1-707-984-6268
Priscilla Mason, Apple Valley, CA,
1-760-961-1997
Stephanie Mosley-McDouglas, Canon, GA,
1-706-356-2343
Wendy Murdoch, New Canaan, CT,
1-203-972-6929
Barbara Owens, Modesto, CA, 1-209-572-4242
Andrea Pabel, Rivera, NM, 1-505-421-3332

Margaret Powell, Goleta, CA, 1-805-964-8414
Marnie Reeder, Austin, TX, 1-512-288-4480
Julie Rubey, Red Oak, IA, 1-712-623-2959
Barbara Stender, Summerfield, NC,
1-336-616-1695
Penny Stone, Spring, TX, 1-512-295-5805
Abby Chew Williams, Belfast, ME,
1-207-338-1117

Practitioner 1

Betsy Adamson, DVM, Redding, CA,
1-916-243-6458
Sally Alasin, Aiken, SC, 1-803-648-4518
Charlie Armour, Fontana, KS, 1-913-849-3635
Cassandra Crowley, Canton, OH,
1-330-493-3663
Mary Gill, Pemberton, NJ, 1-609-894-8175
Shelly Moore, Creswell, OR, 1-541-895-3196
Audrey Johnson, Campton, NH,
1-603-536-2665
Cynthia Reed, Sedona, AZ, 1-520-282-5694
Jan Snodgrass, Upperville, VA,
1-540-364-2377
Jayne Stewart, Albuquerque, NM,
1-505-897-9056

Practitioner

Carolyn Anderson, Seattle, WA,
1-206-368-0610
Julie Bates, Rochester, MI, 1-810-651-3405
Amy Budd, Fort Collins, CO, 1-970-484-2710
Kristi Bush, Martinsville, IN, 1-765-349-1233
Wendy Collins, Hailey, ID, 1-208-788-3029
Irene Downs, Sequim, WA 98382,
1-360-681-4129
Sue English, Wendell, MA, 1-978-544-8969
Shannon Finch, Stanwood, WA,
1-360-629-9641
Ann Finley, Boise, ID, 1-208-336-1485
Jakie Forbes, New Orleans, LA,
1-504-895-5508

Paula Grider, Mooresville, IN, 1-317-261-8150
Shannon Hilliker, Santa Fe, NM,
1-505-986-8476
Linda Holenstein, Bozeman, MT,
1-406-586-1484
Deena Meyer, Inverness, FL, 1-352-637-4311
Diane Moller, Central Point, OR,
1-541-855-9400
Sally Morgan, Northampton, MA,
1-413-586-5058
Helene Muir, Clarksburg, NJ, 1-908-4009-3597
Sandy Rakowitz, Arrington, VA,
1-804-277-8140
Cathy Schreiber, Tucson, AZ, 1-520-531-0195
Suzie Steenbergen, Alpine, CA,
1-619-445-8767
Sally Stephenson, Bingham Frams, MI,
1-810-647-2164
Shelly Swenson, Coquille, OR, 1-541-396-4004
Nancy Taylor, Hailey, ID, 1-208-788-9860
Laura, Verink, Franfort, IL, 1-815-469-3007

Canada

Trainer

Robyn Hood, Vernon, BC, 1-250-545-2336

Instructor

Edie Jane Eaton, Alcove, Quebec,
1-819-459-2110

Practitioner 3

Barbara Janelle, London, ON, 1-519-672-5072
Marion Shearer, Toronto, ON, 1-416-491-6673

Practitioner 2

Phyllis Bauerlein, Edmonton, AB,
1-780-438-3254
Olga Comeau, Hampton, NS, 1-902-665-2101
Sue Faulkner-March, Canmore, AB,
1-403-678-2673

TTEAM INSTRUCTORS AND PRACTITIONERS CONT.

For USA, Canada, UK and Australia

Christine Schwartz, Vernon, BC,
 1-250-545-2336
Tammy Steen, Slocan, BC, 1-250-355-2352

Practitioner 1
Jo Buckland, Winlaw, BC, 1-250-226-7625
Myles Herman, Surrey, BC, 1-250-857-9702
Arlaine Holmes, Forest Grove, BC,
 1-604-857-9702

Practitioner
Carol Cornish, Parksville, BC, 1-250-248-8402
Rose Denko, New Lowell, ON, 1-705-458-0175
Marlene Matson, Quesnel, BC,
 1-250-747-1648
Johanna Rodger, Argyle, MB, 1-204-467-8920
Brenda Senko, Red Deer, AB, 1-403-887-5135
Stephanie Shanahan, Guelph, ON,
 1-519-826-7539
Marie Wellman, Regina, SK, 1-306-757-8027

UK

Practitioner 2
Sarah Fisher, Bath, Somerset, 01761-471182

Practitioner 1
Anne Ashton, Bicester, Oxon, 01869-322372
Christine Booth, Wirral, Merseyside,
 0151-3423001

Lorraine Cookson, Leeds, W. Yorkshire,
 0113-2509808
Susan Groundwell, Salisbury, Wiltshire,
 01722-714384
Margret Murray, County Durham,
 01833-650474
Victoria Jowett, Godalming, Surrey,
 01252-703228
Jo Parkmann, Mixbury, Northants,
 01280-848297
Suella Postles, East Leake, Notts,
 01509-8529479

Practitioner
Tracy Gower, Midhurst, West Sussex,
 01730-814646
Pauline Kermode, Kenilworth, Warwickshire,
 01926-853356
Dawn Minall, Paulton, Bristol, Avon,
 01761-415073
Joy Morris, Cumnor, Oxford, Oxon,
 01865-862272
Caroline Pope, Webheath, Redditch, Worcs,
 01527-546891
Anita Rowe, Tauton, Somerset, 01398-371351
Lucinda Stockley, Bath, Somerset,
 01761-471182
Cathy Tindall, Milton Keynes, Bucks,
 01908-316122
Liesje Webb, Ongar, Essex, 01277-363877
Janet West, Shotley, Suffolk, 01473-787287

Australia

Practitioner 2
Ken and Ro Jelbart, Pakenham, Victoria,
 03-59414800
Catherine Hamber, Kenthurst, NSW,
 02-96541446

Practitioner
Genevieve Stone, Donnybrook, WA,
 08-97316357